Colorblind Racism

Colorblind Racism

Meghan Burke

polity

First published in 2019 by Polity Press

Polity Press
65 Bridge Street
Cambridge CB2 1UR, UK

Polity Press
101 Station Landing
Suite 300
Medford, MA 02155, USA

ISBN-13: 978-1-5095-2441-9 (hardback)
ISBN-13: 978-1-5095-2442-6 (paperback)

A catalogue record for this book is available from the British Library.

Library of Congress Cataloging-in-Publication Data
Names: Burke, Meghan A., author.
Title: Colorblind racism / Meghan Burke.
Other titles: Colourblind racism
Description: Medford, MA : Polity Press, [2018] | Includes bibliographical references and index.
Identifiers: LCCN 2018010022 (print) | LCCN 2018015216 (ebook) | ISBN 9781509524457 (Epub) | ISBN 9781509524419 (hardback) | ISBN 9781509524426 (pbk.)
Subjects: LCSH: United States--Race relations. | Race awareness--United States. | Racism--United States.
Classification: LCC E185.61 (ebook) | LCC E185.61 .B9555 2018 (print) | DDC 305.800973--dc23
LC record available at https://lccn.loc.gov/2018010022

Typeset in 11 on 13 pt Sabon
by Fakenham Prepress Solutions, Fakenham, Norfolk, NR21 8NL
Printed and bound in the United Kingdom by Clays Ltd, Elcograf S.p.A.

For further information on Polity, visit our website: politybooks.com

Contents

Preface

Americans' relationship with racism is an anxious one. Few can deny the realities of our racial past, given the histories of slavery, conquest, Jim Crow, and the Ku Klux Klan. And yet few want to acknowledge the realities of our racial present: deep segregation in our neighborhoods and schools, disparities in wealth and policing, and so much more. Even fewer are willing to explore their own complicity in racial inequalities; many will say that the thing they most fear being called is racist. And so, many reply to the simple claim that black lives *matter* by saying instead that all lives matter – intentionally or otherwise burying the very need to assert that race matters. After all, most of us don't want it to matter – we deeply cherish the ideal of a society where individual qualities are what make or break a person, and don't know what to do with the reality that this is not the society in which we live.

Colorblind racism is fundamentally about denying the reality of ongoing racism, and/or the impact that historical forms of racism still has on the present. It's an ideology – a "common sense" way of looking at the world that explains what we see around us – ongoing advantages for white people and barriers and violence toward people of color. It's ideological because it makes these realities too neat and clean

– some people don't work hard enough, aren't respectful, don't have the right values, etc. And it's ideological because it takes race and racism off the table for these considerations; it won't let us recognize race and racism because to do so would radically change the way so many of us make sense of the world. It would also change the way we see our country, our schools, our workplaces, and our selves.

However, once we can get over this hurdle, we can see why we should, and must, pay attention to race and racism. We can see not only the deep barriers and pain that racism causes for those disadvantaged by it, but also ways, even if seemingly small, that we might be able to leverage some of our own personal and institutional power to make things better. This is difficult work, which many of us do not want to do, lest we come to reckon with our own complicity in an unfair and violent system. But it is necessary, in order for us to realize our shared humanity and to protect our shared futures.

This book will explore this phenomenon of colorblind racism – the ways in which failing to look at race actually advances racism. It will do so first by detailing what is meant by colorblind racism – how it is defined and understood, and how social scientists and others have attempted to study and analyze it. It will then take a deep dive into history, exploring both the history of racism in the United States and how the scholarship around it has both reflected and sought to challenge it. It will also help us to see how we got into this paradox of colorblind racism – a society where removing many overt, state-sponsored forms of racism such as the 'Jim Crow laws' did not in fact eradicate racism, but perhaps made it even harder to name and challenge.

After that, it will canvass what we have been able to learn about colorblind racism: how it lives in our institutions, culture, and interpersonal relationships. A vast body of scholarship has demonstrated the existence of its most common ways of talking and thinking about race, and the impact that this has had on our everyday (and every-night) lives. After that, it will also begin to explore the messier terrain of what are often more complicated ways of making sense of the world around us, and how even our scholarship around colorblind racism has prevented us from seeing most fully the dynamics of contemporary racism and, in some cases, resistance to it. The book concludes with details about some new ways of studying what is sometimes called this "new racism," and some brief notes about how to see and challenge contemporary racism, whether it is colorblind or not.

This book is intended for anyone who has not yet explored this phenomenon deeply – students, teachers, those just entering this area of scholarship, and others. I hope it will also be useful to people who are interested in race and inequality in their communities, schools, places of religious practice, and so on. One short book like this is not meant to tell us everything that is important to know about our racial history or present. However, it is my hope that by scratching this surface, by beginning to see what we often do not wish to see, and by considering how adherence to colorblind ways of talking and thinking about race can be a form of complicity with racism, we will be able to foster new tools for studying and challenging it, and therefore be able to adhere to the ideals that mean so much to us in our world.

Acknowledgments

Writing a book, while a solitary day-to-day practice, is in the end always a community effort. My first thanks go to Kathleen Korgen, who first recommended me for this project and who has also found a number of other ways to amplify my signal as a scholar and to send opportunities my way. From there, Jonathan Skerrett at Polity has been a pure delight to work with, from his first communication offering the opportunity to write this book, to his helpful feedback on the prospectus, and his sharp eye, coupled with warm support, at each stage of the editorial process. Jonathan, as well as Amy Williams toward the end of her time there, Susan Beer for her careful eye on edits, and the rest of the team at Polity, together with peer reviewers, who gave very helpful feedback, are all to be given credit for this book's potential to reach students and scholars and for helping to make this book a resource for those interested in contemporary racism.

I would also like to thank the American Sociological Association's Fund for the Advancement of the Discipline for the grant that first supported a Summit on New Frontiers in the Study of Colorblind Racism, and which brought together leading scholars on colorblindness at Illinois Wesleyan University in Bloomington, Illinois, in May 2016. This collaboration and exchange of ideas represented the best in scholarly discourse and collegial support. I have made an effort to cite and credit the work of the scholars who participated in these conversations throughout the text.

Also, here on my campus, many thanks go to Shireen Shrock in our grants office for coordinating these funds and many of the logistics for this Summit. This research was further supported by a grant from the Illinois Wesleyan University Artistic and Scholarly Development at our Mellon Center. I would also like to thank Avery Amerson, a bright student who helped me to do some of the early work on gathering and annotating sources of this book; Kate Browne for her helpful suggestions about marketing; as well as every student and colleague who respected the neon orange sign on my door that helped me to preserve my daily hour of writing.

Finally, this book is dedicated with love to IWU Posse 1: Shakira Cruz Gonzalez, Quentin Jackson, Pearlie Leaf, Sean Ly, Jarlai Morris, Michael O'Neill, Shaela Phillips, Taylor Robinson, Dareana Roy, and Lizette Toto.

1

Introduction

"I'm not racist. I work with a very successful black man – and he's great!" "It's my grandparents' generation who are the racists. Today anyone can make it if they try hard enough!" *"I don't understand why people play the race card. My family were Swedish immigrants and faced incredible hardships."* "All lives matter." These common sentiments, and more, may, on the surface, seem innocuous – and perhaps even supportive. They seek to validate hard work, they express appreciation for immigrants and some individuals of color, and they purport equal opportunity and fairness – all hallmarks of the American ethos. And yet, each is reflective of what we call colorblind racism.

Colorblind racism asserts that there are no real problems with racism in our society, that challenges stem from individuals rather than our institutions and collective thinking and behavior. In this sense colorblindness is a defense of the status quo. It is also a defense of individuals who may sincerely believe that they operate without bias, or those who believe that no one has any more significant privileges or disadvantages than anyone else. It is the polite talk that isolates some people of color in majority-white spaces, or anyone who wants to talk about race, for fear of discomfort. It is the aggressive pushback to those who *do* discuss the realities of racism and systemic bias and violence in, for example, our criminal justice system.

It is all of these things and more, and it is a core feature of racism in the decades since the Freedom Movement more than fifty years ago in the United States – though it was also present before this time. While "traditional," overt racism has never disappeared, and may in fact be on the rise as the far right is emboldened in many places around the USA and the world, covert, colorblind racism remains prevalent. It is the most popular way of talking and thinking about race in both major US political parties, in most schools, in our legal system, and in our conversations about race. It bends and changes to meet new contexts, but it remains, for now, entrenched. And as such, it is worth exploring what colorblind racism is, how it works, its connection to other forms of racism and studies thereof, its prevalence and manifestations, how it is being modified as times change, and how it is best studied and challenged. That is the purpose of this book.

Definition and Core Features

Colorblind racism typically refers to an assertion of equal opportunity that minimizes the reality of racism in favor of individual or cultural explanations for inequality. There have been several names and bodies of scholarship that have sought to explain the phenomenon; these are explored in a section below. Despite differing conceptualizations, all the related varieties of what we now typically call "colorblind racism" ground the ideology in a broader framework that maintains racial inequality and justifies the ongoing social, economic, and political advantages of being white. As Bonilla-Silva, Lewis, and Embrick (2004) note: "Racial outcomes ... are not the product of individual 'racists' but of the crystallization of racial domination into a racial structure" (558). Colorblind racism, then, folds together ideology and its related material outcomes in a way that justifies racism and white privilege.

It also provides tremendous protection for those who actively harbor racist views, but seek to keep them hidden. This particularly protects the identities and privileges of whites: "One of the things that makes neoliberal racism so difficult to confront is that it takes the overt white supremacy of previous generations and repackages it in a language and context that offer 'plausible deniability' to those who profit from it" (Inwood 2015: 415). Whites who make use of colorblind ideology can therefore not only avert charges of being "a racist," but also come to hold quite genuine, albeit inaccurate, perceptions of the social system. This both legitimates and creates complicity within these systems, allowing unequal systems to persist.

This will perhaps become clearer in an examination of the core features of colorblind racism. While there have been several names given to the phenomenon by scholars, and some slight variations in how the phenomenon is conceptualized and measured, common features seem to rise out of each. First, ideology is used *reactively*, as a means to justify the status quo of racial inequality and white dominance. This can happen through ignorance or denial, but the chief ideological function is always to diminish the explanatory power of racism, either in its legacy from the past or in its perpetuation today (see Feagin 2014). In essence, this feature asserts that the playing field is now equal because laws and policies have eradicated the mechanisms that produce structural inequalities, or because overt racism is less often sanctioned in public, and in many spheres of private, life.

This prevents us from being able to examine *meaningfully* the reality of ongoing racial inequality – something that few dispute, given family wealth structures, deep variations in neighborhood and school conditions, and more. All of these, and many other indicators, are easily measured and regularly demonstrated; the question becomes how they are understood and explained by the ordinary person – or sometimes by powerful people with interests that may be disguised from view. Either way, ignoring our often drastically different starting points towards achieving success, or the prevalence of ongoing forms of racism and bias that persist in everyday life, will necessarily justify inequality. This happens when we, instead, argue that the system itself is fair – that individual efforts and cultural traits are all that matter, or when we ignore or distrust the regular and patterned experiences of those who are marginalized by these systems, preferring inaccurate explanations that perhaps make us more comfortable or that come to be seen as common sense.

The second major feature that arises from the varying conceptualizations of what we now call colorblind racism is its complicity with neoliberal politics and ideologies. This has been traced in some of the most established contemporary theories of racism (see Omi and Winant [1986] 2015) and in the study of how we typically talk about them (Bonilla-Silva and Forman 2000). In fact, one of the early names given to colorblind racism in sociology was "*laissez-faire* racism" (Smith 1995; Bobo, Klugel, and Smith 1997). These neoliberal aspects of colorblind racism include Bonilla-Silva's (2003) "abstract liberalism" frame, discussed in more detail below, which asserts the values of political liberalism: freedom and equality, typically favoring individual competition.

This is deeply connected to notions of meritocracy in the United States, which is both a cherished ideal and, as Heather Beth Johnson (2014) details in her book *The American Dream and the Power of Wealth*, a widely held perception of reality – even when people are simultaneously speaking about the privilege of intergenerational wealth or the realities of discrimination. Other useful analyses of the myth of meritocracy include McNamee and Miller (2009) and Callero (2013) – though there are, of course, countless other logical and empirical claims that also provide robust counterevidence to the notion that we live in a fair society with an equal playing field. Even so, the myth is salient for many, perhaps especially whites, who can derive a positive self-concept from the myths that surround beliefs about merit (see Unzueta, Lowrey, and Knowles 2008), and who sometimes respond to challenges to those beliefs with anger (see Cabrera 2014a).

The final core feature of colorblind racism is its ongoing use of racial stereotypes. This presents a paradox of sorts, given that colorblind racism is meant to deny racism. These stereotypes, however, are often presented as an objective measure of presumed reality (e.g. "Native Americans are alcoholics"), as something to be read positively (e.g. "Asian families teach the value of hard work and academic achievement"), or even sympathetically (Burke 2018) (e.g. "Black children can't succeed because of chaotic home lives"). This core feature allows us to understand how racial myths, racial codes (Hill 2008), and racial storylines are deployed as a common-sense understanding of the contemporary racial landscape, working together with the other frames to advance racism by denying its legacy in bias and intent. While, again, many scholars have traced the emergence of this "new" form of racism, these three shared themes seem to emerge from all of them – providing a distinct form of racism that has worked in tandem with neoliberalism and a post-Civil Rights era.

Discussion Questions

- How familiar do these common themes of colorblind racism sound, from the ways that you've heard race discussed in everyday life?
- Who benefits from a widespread belief in colorblindness?
- What elements of racial inequality are hardest to explain without these "common-sense" notions about race and racism?

Early Studies of the "New" Racism

Much of the research in the post-Civil Rights era has been devoted to changes in the racial system in the United States, and grappled with language to mark the differences that scholars were noting between "traditional" racism – that which was overt and direct – and this "new" racism, which is more covert and abstract. Beginning in the 1970s, many new terms emerged for this phenomenon; an appendix provides a brief chronology of the terminology and associated authors that unfolded in academic scholarship during these years. While these studies are often noting some specific differences that necessitate, in their view, a new term, there is a way in which this collective body of scholarship on symbolic racism, modern racism, covert racism, new racism, and *laissez-faire* racism parsed out phenomena that now constitute the core themes outlined above. A more advanced study of the differences between these terms is possible; the appendix can provide a roadmap for such endeavors. And, even here, some important differences will be highlighted. Even so, an overview of scholarship around colorblind racism excavates the themes that came out of these decades of scholarship. Doing this both acknowledges where the research has been focused and helps us to understand how the scholarship has crystalized around "colorblind racism" as the most widely used framework today. This brief overview will also help us to appreciate why sociologists (and many others) prefer a framework that pairs those beliefs and their expressions with real social outcomes.

What we now call colorblind racism seems to have first been identified by social psychologists. In 1970, Joel Kovel named the "aversive" racist as "the type who believes in white race superiority but does nothing overt about it" (1970: 54), placing it as a transitional type between the "dominative" racist and a non-racist. Kovel's analysis is deeply psycho-analytical, depending on notions of an unconscious hatred or resentment, and does not seem to have gained much traction for empirical study. After all, our unconscious drives are by definition buried from view and one's own awareness. They are, however, sometimes reflected in attitudes of resentment, and psychology as a discipline has paid close attention to these racial attitudes and how they may best be measured – for example, in the development of a modern racism scale (McConahay, Hardee, and Batts 1981).

These measures and scales begin to give us a picture of how attitudes about race may operate in tandem with political behavior and correlate with other belief systems, but many sociologists find them limiting. After all, a focus on individual beliefs and attitudes, using a scale that parses "racists" from non-racists, will fail to see how we can all participate in systems of racial inequality, and even *sincerely* operate on the basis of faulty knowledge when doing so. Further, in his critique of psychological frameworks for studying racism, Bonilla-Silva (1997) argues that:

> If racism is not part of a society but is a characteristic of individuals who are "racist" or "prejudiced" – that is, racism is a phenomenon operating at the individual level – then (1) social institutions cannot be racist and (2) studying racism is simply a matter of surveying the proportion of people in a society who hold "racist" beliefs. (467)

And so, while individual attitudes and beliefs are also important in sociology, they are not alone sufficient for understanding how and why racial inequality persists; this involves much more than prejudice. Even so, these early studies – largely psychological, but also coming from political science and some other sociologists – give us a picture of some of the early themes that characterize this "new" racism, and connect to how we now understand colorblind racism.

Abstract Values

The first among these themes is that manifestations of racism – or in some cases, simply talk about racism – takes on an abstract nature that is focused on values and morality rather than specific traits about groups of people. They may focus, instead, on "the kind of traditional American moral values embodied in the Protestant Ethic" (cited in Kinder and Sears 1981: 416). These are notions about hard work, austerity and delayed gratification, individual merit, and equality – often by imagining that we already have a society where equal opportunity truly exists, and is not, for example, shaped by family wealth, quality of neighborhood schools, or patterns of discrimination. Instead, the abstract nature of this "new" racism involves "abstract moral assertions about blacks' behavior as a group, concerning what blacks deserve, how they ought to act, whether or not they are treated equitably, and so on" (Sears and McConahay 1973: 138–9). While the focus on black people is an important characteristic – explored in the next section – these claims attempt legitimacy by focusing on values themselves rather than the (often imagined) behavior of groups who (again, we imagine) do not adhere to these principles.

This is exactly how McConahay and Hough defined "symbolic racism" in 1976, when they wrote that it is "the expression in terms of abstract ideological symbols and symbolic behaviors of the feeling that blacks are violating cherished values and making illegitimate demands for changes in the racial status quo" (38). We see this today in concerns about the welfare system – as many Americans, despite ongoing evidence to the contrary, believe that African Americans abuse a system designed to help what is sometimes thought of as the more deserving poor – though poor people in the United States are often thought to be undeserving, given those same values around hard work and individual merit (see Katz [1989] 2013). The way that these values are tapped also appears in Pettigrew and Meertens's (1995) definition of "subtle racism": "a defense of traditional values ... [an] exaggeration of cultural differences... [and a] denial of positive emotions [toward an outgroup]" (58–9). McConahay's (1986) research argues that this focus on values sometimes also creates ambivalence for people who may be torn between a desire to adhere to values of egalitarianism and fairness, which comes into conflict with anti-black attitudes and beliefs.

Either way, the focus on values and morality constitutes a core feature of both early and contemporary conceptualisms of post-Civil Rights era racism. We call this an *abstract* focus on morals and values because in some ways discussions of "equality" and the "value" of hard work are necessarily abstract concepts – ideals to which we might aspire, or against which we might compare ourselves at either a social or individual level. More importantly, however, these are *abstract* values because they specifically do *not* reflect reality. Decades of research continually echo what most people of color will tell any white person who is willing to listen – that whites often receive unfair advantages and that opportunities are not equal given the structure of family wealth, neighborhood and school segregation, and ongoing racial discrimination. And so, while we can abstractly assert the value of equal opportunity, hard work, and more – these notions are just that: not grounded in real, measurable, and persistent inequalities.

Anti-Blackness

Of course, as the previous section makes clear, these abstract values are rarely asserted independently of the associated racist belief that some racial groups, most often black Americans, are deficient in their ability to live up to these cherished ideals. Most studies, as we also saw above, situate them as co-existing beliefs (see Sears and McConahay 1973; Kinder and Sears 1981). They write, "Symbolic racism represents a form of resistance to change in the racial status quo based on moral feelings that blacks violate such traditional American values as individualism and self-reliance, the work ethic, obedience, and discipline" (Kinder and Sears 1981: 416). In much of their work (including in their earliest work in 1971), Sears and Kinder emphasize early socialization and social distance in perpetuating white racist fears and, in their view, a resulting inclination toward conservative politics.

In that sense, while colorblind racism is not a weapon wielded exclusively against black Americans, it has often included a sharp focus on the often-imagined traits of black Americans. Bobo, Kluegel, and Smith's (1997) concept of *laissez-faire* racism "involves persistent negative stereotyping of African Americans, a tendency to blame blacks themselves for the black–white gap in socioeconomic standing, and resistance to meaningful policy efforts to ameliorate US racist social conditions and institutions" (16). These efforts most often include affirmative action policies, which simply try to assure equal opportunities, and spending for a social safety net – mitigating some of the harshest impacts of wealth and income inequality.

All such policy efforts have been deeply tainted by pervasive yet unfounded racist imagery of black Americans as immoral, lazy, and seeking unwarranted recognition. There are several excellent books that detail the history of how this imagery became so pervasive, particularly as it has become attached to policy debates. One is Jill Quadagno's (1994) *The Color of Welfare*, which traces the myth of the "welfare queen" and how deeply racism has impacted changes in the welfare system in decades past. Another is Herbert Gans's (1995) *The War Against the Poor*. While both of those books are by now decades old, they remain useful in detailing how these notions about black and/or poor Americans, which we typically take for granted, came to be mobilized and paired with political power to cement both anti-black racism and ongoing structural disadvantages. Today, anti-blackness is pervasive as ever, as we see in strong aversion to the Black Lives Matter movement and other symbols of empowerment, in attacks on social services spending, and in persistent media distortions.

Covert Nature

Of course, while overt racism persists, in many cases this anti-blackness (or other kinds of racism like the model minority stereotype, notions about race and immigration or national security, and more) tends to take on a covert nature. This is another defining feature of research into racism in the post-Civil Rights era. In fact, in some ways, this subtle or covert nature may be its hallmark characteristic, as is evident in the title of Robert C. Smith's (1995) book *Racism in the Post-Civil Rights Era: Now You See It, Now You Don't*. This ambivalent nature of modern racism also involves a closer attention to rhetoric and discourse, for example in Bonilla-Silva and Forman's (2000) investigation into the ways of speaking about race "that allow [whites] to safely voice racial views that might be otherwise interpreted as racist" (68–9). This covert, modern, subtle racism, as social psychologists variously termed it, is "cool, distant, indirect" (Pettigrew and Meertens 1995: 58).

In some ways this distance is achieved through a focus, as we have already explored, on its abstract nature. Notions about equal opportunity, hard work, and self-reliance are often preferred over direct discussion about the racial groups who are imagined to break with those norms and values. Coded racism is another strategy used to convey racial logic without using racist expressions. When we talk about "thugs" or "gangbangers," or when we rail against "illegal immigrants" or "welfare queens" or "terrorists," we are not naming any specific racial group. But we are talking about deeply racially loaded topics where specific racial imagery supports racist ideas about who these categories of people are understood to be. So, in this way, what we now call colorblind racism is indirect: it is the color-*blind* part that holds up the system of racism – one of the persistent racist stereotypes and structures and institutions that allow racial inequalities to persist.

Institutions and Social Structures

A focus on those structures and institutions, then, is the final feature of research into this new form of racism. Smith's (1995) book, mentioned above, traced the historical evolution of racism in the United States, and challenged the literature about the "underclass" – language given to those who experience persistent poverty and come to survive outside of the formal economic system (see Wilson 1987). His book instead emphasizes the realities of institutional racism, as did Bobo, Klugel, and Smith's (1997) concept of *laissez-faire* racism. Both studies explored the historical and material basis of racism, and articulated a sociological, rather than a social psychological, theory of prejudice. Bobo, Klugel, and Smith (1997) write, "This framework is one that takes seriously the imperatives that derive from both the institutionalized structural conditions of social life as well as from the process of human interaction, subjectivity, and interpretation that lend meaning to social conditions and thereby guide behavior" (22). It is in this sense that they also emphasize that "*laissez-faire* racist attitudes emerged to defend white privilege and explain persistent black disadvantage under sharply changed [from older, Jim Crow] economic and political conditions" (ibid.). This sharp focus on privilege helps us to see beyond individual attitudes and beliefs and instead to peer into the realities of how social systems work beyond individual intent.

While those studies were published in the late 1990s, the first sociological treatment of what we now call color-blind racism may be Mary Jackman's body of scholarship that emphasizes contemporary racism's deep connections to privilege: "Instead of treating intergroup attitudes as shreds of anachronistic parochialism, we regard them as an integral part of the ideologies that privileged social groups routinely develop to legitimize and protect their interests within the status quo" (Jackman and Muha 1984). This was perhaps the beginning of an ongoing trajectory of research and theorizing that sought to understand ideology as an important engine for a changing social structure (Omi and Winant [1986] 2015). It is similarly in this spirit that sociologist Ruth Frankenberg (1993) discussed a move from "essentialist" – hierarchical and biological – forms of racism to

a discourse of essential sameness popularly referred to as 'color-blindness' – which I have chosen to name as a double move toward 'color evasiveness' and 'power evasiveness.' This ... asserts that we are all the same under the skin; that, culturally, we are converging; that, materially, we have the same chances in US society; and that – the sting of the tail – any failure to achieve is therefore the fault of people of color themselves. (14)

Frankenberg's framework, which focuses on power and scorn, is among the earliest sociological frameworks to articulate a "colorblind" racism – encompassing all of the features above and moving beyond individual attitudes and psyches to locate power relations in systems and institutions that impact on individuals beyond interactions.

Terminology

As the above themes make clear, what we now call color-blind racism has been given a number of names in the past several decades. Even as far back as 1981, McConahay et al. wrote, "Previous work with the concept of modern racism has termed it 'symbolic racism' .... The label was changed from symbolic to modern racism in order to emphasize the contemporary, post-Civil Rights Movement nature of the beliefs and issues" (564–5). This is around the same time that Pettigrew (1979) also began, following a similar logic, calling it "new" racism – though Pettigrew would again call it "modern" racism in 1989. The first book title popularizing the term was Leslie G. Carr's (1997) *"Color-Blind" Racism*, where he also emphasized its role as a racist ideology. The term was further popularized in this same year by journalist Ellis Cose, whose book *Color-Blind: Seeing Beyond Race in a Race-Obsessed World* explored the contradictions and tensions of the post-Civil Rights era.

Eduardo Bonilla-Silva, Amanda Lewis, and David Embrick (2004) defend their choice to use the term colorblind racism, rather than relying on past conceptualizations of symbolic or modern racism, "because it fits better how whites talk about race in the post-Civil Rights era.... Rather than basing this perspective on whites' 'attitudes,' we argue this viewpoint represents a new ideological formation and use textual rather than survey data to document it" (558). Although many sociological studies have followed from these foundations (O'Brien 2000; Gallagher 2003; Brown et al. 2003 – and all those discussed in Chapter 3), most now share an emphasis on colorblindness as an ideological framework, and its associated material consequences. The term seems to have stuck, and is easily the most common one used in research from the 2000s onward.

Discussion Questions

- Which of the previous names given to colorblind racism do you think best captures its defining features?
- Which elements of colorblind racism uncovered by this body of scholarship seem most important to emphasize?
- What features of contemporary racism, if any, seem to be missing in this shift toward analyses of colorblind racism?

Bonilla-Silva's *Racism Without Racists*

In sociology, it is Eduardo Bonilla-Silva (2003) whose work has had the greatest impact, despite these varying early attempts to name the phenomenon. While his 2001 book *White Supremacy and Racism in the Post-Civil Rights Era,* along with some of his other early work (e.g. Bonilla-Silva and Forman 2000), began to trace these threads, it is in his 2003 *Racism Without Racists: Color-Blind Racism and the Persistence of Racial Inequality in America* where his theory about colorblind racism receives its most direct and extensive treatment. This book, now in its fifth edition, is read widely by students in undergraduate and graduate classrooms, and has been cited thousands of times. Bonilla-Silva, therein, asserts that this ideology "explains contemporary racial inequality as the outcome of nonracial dynamics" (2003: 2). His book also establishes four central frames, or "set paths for interpreting information" (2003: 26), that have been useful in identifying this ideology.

Abstract Liberalism

Abstract liberalism is the first of these frames, and the one that Bonilla-Silva calls the "most important, as it constitutes the foundation of the new racial ideology" (2003: 26).

Abstract liberalism presumes the existence of a meritocratic system – thus the "liberalism" component. It is based on the ideals of equal opportunity and individual merit and competition. And yet it asserts this ideal as though it were not an ideal at all, but rather a reality. This provides its' "abstract" nature. As Bonilla-Silva writes, "By framing race-related issues in the language of liberalism, whites can appear 'reasonable' and even 'moral' while opposing almost all practical approaches to deal with *de facto* racial inequality. For instance, by using the tenets of the free market ideology in the abstract, they can oppose affirmative action as a violation of the norm of equal opportunity" (28).

This frame is ideological because it ignores the persistent structural and institutional inequalities, alongside the strong anti-black and other racist notions, that prevent the tenets of liberalism from being achieved. Take, for example, the realities of family wealth. As Johnson details in her (2014) book *The American Dream and the Power of Wealth*, not only does family wealth directly counter the principles of a meritocracy – where one competes for and earns wealth on an equal playing field – but such wealth is dramatically unevenly patterned by race; most studies find something between eight and twelve times the wealth in white families when compared to black families. There is a preponderance of research tracing this pattern – one classic is Oliver and Shapiro's (2006) *Black Wealth, White Wealth*. In this sense, opportunities – for decent housing and schools, the foundation for most further success – are vastly unequal; yet abstract liberalism asserts a fair system of earned advantages, independent of the realities of race.

Naturalization

The second central frame is naturalization, which, as Bonilla-Silva writes, "allows whites to explain away racial phenomena by suggesting that they are natural occurrences" (2003: 28). This seems most often to appear in the contexts of segregation, both of physical spaces like neighborhoods and for social spaces such as friend and family groups. By asserting that it is "only natural" that "like attracts like," it reinforces abstract liberalism by deflating racist practices (or the outcomes thereof) as a matter of choice and preference. This also makes use of a faulty logic that claims that since people of color may also demonstrate in-group preferences, the playing field is indeed a level one. Human beings, it says, regardless of race, assert preferences that are seen to be if not entirely biological, then at least anthropological: that is, it is a core element of human behavior.

While certainly individuals do have choices, naturalization is ideological in that it removes the possibility and reality of racial (and other) biases that impact those preferences and choices, or the structural and institutional barriers that prevent an individual's ability to act on that choice. And so, neighborhood "preference" is also, as much research suggests, about racial preference (see, for example, Bader and Krysan 2015); the same is true for friendship and other social networks (see e.g. Kao and Joiner 2004; Bonilla-Silva and Embrick 2007). And while it is true that people of color may also elect social spaces that are segregated by race, their reasons for doing so are often a reaction to a racist system that makes such spaces a place of refuge and restoration (for an excellent, accessible treatment of this phenomenon, see Beverly Tatum's (1997) *Why are all The Black Kids Sitting Together in the Cafeteria? And Other Conversations About Race*). As such, there is nothing "natural" about these preferences – they are created as a result of our social systems and practices.

Cultural Racism

The third central frame that Bonilla-Silva articulates for colorblind racism is what he calls cultural racism, which "relies on culturally based arguments such as 'Mexicans do not put much emphasis on education' or 'blacks have too many babies' to explain the standing of minorities in society" (2003: 28). As I often tell students, this is the frame that sounds the most traditionally racist; what makes it color-blind is that it no longer makes assertions about inherent or biological differences but rather favors presumably learned differences.

One would think that given its categorical nature, this frame would be the easiest to challenge, but instances of this frame often do not seem racist to the speaker, but rather are believed to be accurate depictions of cultural differences. Of course, these beliefs are neither accurate nor are they alone sufficient to explain success or failure. The example of the "model minority" stereotype, which explains rates of greater economic and educational attainment among Asians by saying that 'Asian culture' emphasizes hard work and academics more so than the cultures of other people of color in the United States, demonstrates this fallacy well. For one, most family and cultural systems emphasize hard work and academic success; first-generation immigrants emphasize this for their children even more (Chiswick and DebBurman 2004). Asians were largely barred from immigrating to the United States in any substantial numbers from 1880 until 1965, when changes in our immigration laws favored individuals with specific skill sets in math and science and drew from a backlog of eligible populations in Asia in order to do so. Prior to this, it was feared that Asians were *not smart enough* to be in the United States, and would harm the country as a result. As I tell my students, Asians didn't change; our laws and policies did. And so, while it's true that many Asian families teach their children the value of hard work and academic success, they do not do so exclusively; nor does this alone explain their aggregate success in these industries.

Minimization of Racism

The final central frame of colorblind racism is the minimization of racism frame. While together all of the frames, as well as the storylines and other discursive maneuvers of colorblind racism, minimize racism, this one does so directly. It either suggests that racial bias has diminished in its impact on the life chances and experiences of people of color, or it favors alternate explanations, such as social class or a lack of direct agency, in explaining away racial phenomena. Examples include the direct assertion that someone, or something, is not racist; the (usually obvious) fact that someone didn't own slaves; the wishful belief that "the past is the past" and therefore that none of its institutional or ideological legacies remain; or that people of color are playing "the race card" to gain favor in a given situation – as if racism and its consequences can be reduced to a game.

These four frames are now pervasive in a range of sociological studies testing for the existence of colorblind racism; Chapter 3 canvasses the literature where they have been documented in service of ongoing racial inequality in a wide range of settings. That said, Chapters 4 and 5 also reveal that an exclusive focus on finding and documenting these frames can obscure other important manifestations and modifications of colorblind racism that still work in service of white supremacy and ongoing racial inequality. Even so, their deep familiarity to most listeners who learn to use them, as well as the vast scholarship that has built on Bonilla-Silva's articulation of them as frames, has been tremendously helpful in advancing the scholarship to date.

Discussion Questions

- What are some specific familiar phrases that reflect these four frames?
- How can your growing capacity as a sociological thinker counter some of those frames when you encounter them in everyday life?

Methods of Study

While by now widely studied, systematically documenting and analyzing colorblindness is not without its methodological challenges. As Angie Beeman (2015) writes, "scholars of color-blind ideology face a unique challenge, because they are investigating the seeming absence of a phenomenon rather than the presence of it" (143). Of course, the key word is "seeming," as the symbolic nature of colorblindness, as well as the core features discussed earlier in this chapter, can all be operationalized, and their presence traced carefully. Still, there is considerable debate about the best way to do this, and tremendous variation in how to best do so among academic disciplines. Social psychologists, when they were developing their "symbolic" and "modern" racism scales, relied exclusively on attitudinal surveys, attempting to trace causality between these colorblind beliefs and political orientation, various racial attitudes, and support for race-relevant policies. These studies often produced shaky results, but tended to suggest coherence with conservatism and racial prejudice. Psychologists have also developed a Colorblind Racial Attitude Scale, or CoBRAS (Neville et al. 2000).

As Bonilla-Silva and Dietrich (2011) write, "Although conceptually different, the CoBRAS measure of color-blind racism was positively correlated with many measures of racial prejudice. Other studies have found that the CoBRAS measure of color-blind racism was positively correlated with white fear of other races" (194).

In sociology, most colorblindness studies tend to employ qualitative methods, perhaps given the discursive focus of Bonilla-Silva's (2003) book. In fact, therein, he suggests that qualitative methods are best suited to study the phenomenon, because "survey questions still restrict the free flow of ideas and unnecessarily constrain the range of possible answers for respondents" (11). These methods include analyses of interview data, content analysis of both private and public discourse, field observation, and more. However, there have been effective strategies for studying colorblindness using quantitative methods in sociology. Paul Croll (2013) used quantitative methods to explore whites' understanding of racial advantage, suggesting that "far greater numbers of Americans see ways in which whites benefit from racialized systems than may have been previously assumed" (70).

No matter the discipline or method of study, as Chapter 3 will explore, the relationship between colorblind racial attitudes and/or discourses and a variety of social phenomena is well demonstrated. And in most cases this relationship upholds rather than challenges the status quo of deep racial inequality and related notions of white supremacy in the United States and in many other places around the world. This is not to say that colorblindness is the only form of racism, or that direct and clearly hostile racism does not persist. It simply suggests that given how colorblind racism has taken a deep hold on our public and private lives, it has been clearly identified and widely studied by social scientists, whose task is to better understand those lives.

The Rise and Fall of "Post-Racial" Politics: Race and Contemporary Politics

While many have conceptualized colorblindness as a "new" form of racism, it is crucial to emphasize that overt forms of racism have not disappeared. Rather, they may have simply moved out of the public eye, and into the "backstage" (Picca and Feagin 2007; Hughey 2011). Raúl Pérez (2017), for example, has studied the existence of startlingly explicit racism expressed as humor defiant of the pressures to be "politically correct," which is anything but colorblind. While some of this takes place in anonymous forums online, humorists, comedians, and political groups such as the alt-right often make use of racist humor to build camara-derie and to support white supremacy. Kristen Myers (2005) has also documented widespread overt racism among college students, who are typically thought to be more progressive and enlightened than older generations.

Journalists also noted a rise in activity among race-based hate groups after the election of Barack Obama (see Zeskind 2012). Hate crimes also surged after the election of Donald Trump; the Southern Poverty Law Center (2016) reported, "In the ten days following the election, there were almost 900 reports of harassment and intimidation from across the nation. Many harassers invoked Trump's name during assaults, making it clear that the outbreak of hate stemmed in large part from his electoral success" (4). Further, these reported events do *not* include online forms of harassment or bullying, where they are surely more pervasive.

It is perhaps for this reason that Feagin ([2006] 2013) has documented a centuries-old white racial frame, an "organized set of racialized ideas, stereotypes, emotions, and inclinations to discriminate" (227). While some of these are colorblind, some remain explicitly racist in nature, passed down through common-sense notions, socialized in families and an array of public spaces, and practiced widely among institutions. Perhaps even more insidious is what Tyrone Forman (2004) has conceptualized as racial apathy, a concept that "captures the ways in which whites may publicly express indifference or lack of care about racial inequality while at the same time continuing to hold anti-minority views" (51). Others practice what Matthew Oware (2016) has called racial evasion:

> ... defined as (1) superficially referencing race, but not deliberately engaging or articulating racial dynamics, and (2) readily avoiding involved discussions surrounding racism occurring at the institutional or individual level that are quite obviously racial (through their history, construction, or manifestation). (374)

All of the above practices protect the identity and comfort of whites at the expense of people of color and/or further engagement with antiracist efforts. Perhaps this is why, as Angie Beeman (2015) notes: "The main problem with the term color-blind racism is that it conflates two separate concepts, the ideology of colorblindness and systemic racism of which it is itself a part" (130). A wave of current research, explored in Chapter 4, further unpacks this possibility. Either way, it should be noted that colorblindness does not necessarily constitute all contemporary race talk. But it does continue to drive its center and its ability to relate to the mainstream (Burke 2012a), and for this reason is continually important to study.

Discussion Questions

- What proportion of the race talk that you observe is overt? Where does it occur, and by whom?
- Given the wide range of expressions of racism, how do you think it is best measured and studied?

The Urgency of New Frontiers

As I have argued elsewhere (Burke 2016), too often the research on colorblind racism has focused only on documenting the presence of colorblind racism, at the expense of a more detailed analysis of the ways that this form of racism may be connected to the individuals and institutions that surround it, and to the ever-changing realities of racial ideologies as the social structure around us also morphs and changes. We need to continually delve deeper into the concrete mechanisms that produce and reconstitute contemporary racism, particularly colorblindness, so that we may learn more about, and better challenge, these systems of oppression.

For example, how and why is a barely coded racial logic appealing to those on the far right, and why are those on the left also often unwilling to disrupt its core logic? When people talk about "illegal" immigrants or welfare cheats, they are ostensibly talking about law and policy, but with deeply racially coded inferences about those who are, they imagine, a threat. How might we also reconcile a desire for colorblindness, or what some scholars (Hartman et al. 2017) are calling a colorblind identity, with the belief in colorblindness as an ideology? In other words, if someone says that they are colorblind, this can be an expression of moral commitment to antiracism as much as it can be a defense of the racist status quo. Another line of questioning asks how colorblindness is modified or abandoned when social configurations differ. This allows us to explore more deeply how the use of this discourse varies among people of color, in different political spaces, in diverse or non-diverse settings. Finally, to ask what new insights might these dynamics reveal about contemporary racism, so that social justice may prevail. The later chapters of this book will delve into these questions, and more.

After all, colorblind racism is often framed as a way of making sense of the ongoing reality of racial inequality that persists after the gains of the Civil Rights Movement of the 1950s and 1960s. Chapter 2 will help readers to situate the eventual emergence of what we now call "colorblind" racism in historical context. It will also trace some of the past treatments of racism in the social sciences as they relate to major events in United States history, so that the trajectory into contemporary, colorblind racism will become more apparent. It will, further, explore the reality that color-blind racism is not entirely a feature of the *post*-Civil Rights United States; it has both ideological and discursive footings that have facilitated its full emergence as a later feature of the twentieth-century racial landscape. For this reason, it is worth considering this era for its own discursive shifts, including but not limited to the reframing of the Freedom Movement into a movement for "Civil Rights." This era is also defined by the Cold War, and as such, this chapter will consider the co-evolution of neoliberalism and US dominance alongside the domestic struggles for racial and social justice. It will conclude with clarity about what the Civil Rights Movement did and did not achieve, which will help readers to better understand how racial inequality can continue to grow despite these important legal victories.

Given the large body of literature that has emerged since the development of this framework, it will then be important for Chapter 3 to canvass what we know about colorblind racism from the contributions of the social sciences – not just in sociology but also in law, psychology, education, criminal justice, medicine, and political science. This chapter provides an overview of these findings; in particular, it will highlight the mobilization of colorblind ideology and discourse in institutions, policy, culture, and interpersonal settings. In this sense, this is the chapter that best surveys where color-blind ideology has been used to support racial inequality and its persistence.

And yet, despite the wide array of instances where color-blindness is deployed, it is far from monolithic. Chapter 4 will explore the myriad ways that colorblindness is modified or abandoned by a range of social actors with varying social and political goals. It also, crucially, emphasizes that the emergence of this "new" racism has not meant an abandonment of the "old," that overt or other traditional forms of racism have themselves persisted or been modified in ways that complicate our understanding of how ideology and discourse interact with our social and political systems in order to shape outcomes and advantages in a diverse racial landscape. It concludes by raising questions about the framework of colorblindness itself, setting the stage for the concluding chapter that follows.

Finally, given the reality of the divergences and complex-ities in the chapter that precedes it, Chapter 5 will trace the emergence of new research that is seeking to better understand contemporary racism, and to advance our under-standing of colorblindness from eras past. This includes new research that is beginning to parse out colorblind discourse from a colorblind identity, what it might look like to retain colorblindness as an ideal as opposed to a reality, and research that dives deeper into the complexities and contradictions of colorblindness alongside competing racial frameworks. The chapter will conclude with a vision for better understanding contemporary, colorblind racism and the tools that may be valuable in challenging it.

It is never easy to confront the realities of racism that shape our social systems, particularly given contemporary pressures not to discuss race in the first place. Many who care deeply about equality will still struggle to name and talk about racial realities like inequality, bias, mistreatment, violence, and more, because they fear either being perceived as racist or "playing the race card." Even the notion that race can exist as a playing card trivializes race and racism as serious and central components that shape advantages and disadvantages, and the full range of experiences in our everyday lives. This is the very essence of colorblindness, and the racism that it can so often help to reproduce makes choosing to study it, name it, talk about it, and act to change it so vital. This is our task in the chapters that follow.

Further Exploration

- Spend the next week documenting all instances where you hear or read about race and racism being discussed. Are these instances colorblind or overt? Are they coded? Where does each type take place, and by whom?

2

Colorblindness in Historical Context

On a basic level, colorblindness refers to the move from overt to covert racist expressions, or from direct to perhaps indirect or even unintentional forms of degradation and/or racial exclusion. It is also reflective of the changing nature of the legal system brought about by the Civil Rights Movement of the 1950s and 1960s, where institutional forms of racism moved from explicit to tacit forms. So, while in many ways it makes sense to consider the Civil Rights era as a turning point, there are at least two important ways in which the characteristics of US racism are more fluid, historically, than the focus on the 1960s first presumes. After all, as Bonilla-Silva noted in his 1997 piece, "The form of race relations – overt or covert – depends on the pattern of racialization that structures a particular society" (468). Closely examining the changes in the US social structure around race, as the idea of race itself also evolved, will also allow us to see how colorblindness emerged, and how the scholarship around it changed in response.

The Evolution of US Racism

Colorblind racism is a framework for making sense of the

ongoing reality of racial inequality that persists after the gains of the US Civil Rights Movement of the 1950s and 1960s. It is beyond the scope of this chapter to explore fully the history of the idea of race, and therefore of racism, in the United States. Those interested in such histories can turn to Omi and Winant's *Racial Formation in the United States* ([1986] 2015), Feagin's *White Party, White Government* (2012), and the many other sources that I will briefly integrate along the way. Still, it is worth spending some time deliberately considering how this ostensibly "new" era of colorblindness has historical footing in eras past, while also examining its changes over time.

Pre-Civil Rights Racism

Colorblind racism is at its core a contradiction – it is color-blind, and yet it is racist. Nowhere is this contradiction more clear than in the foundational claim that "all men are created equal," written by white men, some of whom held other human beings as property. Debates over the abolition of slavery eventually led to a civil war. And while slavery was ultimately abolished, the debates about slavery were not always explicitly about the direct subjugation of black bodies, but rather over what scientifically qualified someone as human, or about states' rights. On the former count, what we often call "scientific racism" emerged as biologists and other natural scientists began to assert hierarchies within the human race – always justifying the white supremacist practices of slavery and colonialism. This use of science, all of which has since been discredited, was also applied in the use of eugenics, a deadly practice of similarly creating legitimations for racial or ethnic supremacy, and fostering practices designed to sustain an imagined purity of the "white" race. Examples of eugenics practices range from the biological belief in Aryan superiority used in the Holocaust to anti-miscegenation laws (opposing interracial marriage) and forced sterilization of those deemed unfit to reproduce, such as black, native, and Latina women. While the science supporting hierarchies among human beings has long since been abandoned, this debate over the criteria for humanity, rather than greed and racial exploitation, followed a color-blind logic.

The debate over states' rights, of course, is much the same, and persists in much political debate today, including in spaces that reflect and reproduce racial inequality such as voting and housing. As Crespino (2007) writes:

> In the late nineteenth century, exclusionary provisions in the 1890 Mississippi state constitution – statutes that led to the systematic disenfranchisement of black voters and the social subjugation of African Americans – were framed in language that made no explicit reference to race. Segregationists' most familiar defense – states' rights – was a color-blind argument as well, one that couched the defense of white supremacy in terms of political principle rather than racial superiority. (8–9)

In many ways, this is the same as Bonilla-Silva's abstract liberalism frame, one of the four central frames of colorblind racism. Recall that abstract liberalism shifts the discourse and grounds for debate to abstract principles such as equality, competition, autonomy, and others, and away from the real and deeply racially unequal contexts in which such principles are forged. This perhaps explains the reason why, after the Civil War, the South was racially hostile and utilized exclusionary tactics like Jim Crow laws, while the North was ambivalent but institutionally more accommodating.

This Southern hostility quickly stamped down efforts made by freed black people in the era of Reconstruction, from the end of the Civil War in 1865 until 1877, where gains were quickly made toward some reasonable accommodations for freed African Americans in housing, education, employment, and more. Southern whites soon responded to this progress by organizing the Ku Klux Klan and other forms of racial terror, and through the piecemeal but rapid implementation of Jim Crow laws and policies. These strategies had as their premise a deep desire for racial exclusion and a preservation of imagined white purity, but were defended by using the logic of "states' rights," personal liberty, and protecting one's property. Similarly, Alien Land Acts prevented non-citizens from owning land in many Western states – a policy based on anti-Asian discrimination but forged under citizens-first language.

It is perhaps Jim Crow racism that made use most actively of overt strategies to enforce white supremacy, primarily by explicitly marking space and other resources as the exclusive property of whites via active racial segregation. Examples include signs marking public and private places for "whites only" as well as active, legal efforts to block people of color from schools, neighborhoods, and more. It also emerged in our immigration laws in the form of the Chinese Exclusion Act and in our policy to preserve homesteading opportunities in the developing American West exclusively for whites, and not for indigenous peoples who had long claimed the land. This suppressed the opportunities for racially marginalized Americans to gain wealth, education, and dignity. It also, crucially, allowed whites to hoard considerable amounts of wealth. They did so both in the exclusive housing markets that they created, where the most desirable properties and therefore those that can best appreciate in value over time were available exclusively to whites, as well as in family systems that continued to transfer this wealth between generations. In this way, even well-meaning whites who may harbor less racial hatred could still benefit from these systemic injustices.

These benefits were further supported by New Deal reforms, undertaken in response to the Great Depression, which created tremendous opportunities for employment and security for large numbers of white Americans – albeit in a colorblind fashion. This jobs effort and the safety net that it created were a boon for whites, who could either climb the economic ladder into the middle class or sustain their position if they were already there. However, these New Deal reforms rarely were made available to people of color, who were excluded by their concentration in occupational categories like farmworkers, domestic servants, and others. These New Deal reforms also did not prevent unions from continuing their longstanding practice to lock black and brown workers out, and therefore left them without access to the protections and pensions that helped to create a strong, white middle class. However, even here, the overt logic for racial exclusion was created by occupation and the ability of unions to administer their own affairs without governmental regulation, rather than explicitly by racism.

As such, as Cedric de Leon (2011) argues, "the United States since 1932 has witnessed a gradual unfolding of a regime of race relations grounded in colorblind ideology" (80). Roediger (2008) makes a similar claim:

> The [New Deal] reformers often claimed to be administering race-neutral or colorblind programs, even as their deference to local racist practices left Jim Crow intact. Liberalism's appeals to race neutrality were twofold. First job growth, union organization, and relief could be said to benefit all of the poor, thereby justifying a strategy of progressing on economic fronts without emphasizing racial justice. Secondly, even the most glaring omissions of people of color from economic reform programs took on race-neutral forms. (176)

It is perhaps for this reason that this era also began to see a gradual shift from a focus on whites' ethnic status (as Irish, Jewish, Italian, etc.) to that of their race (as *whites*). It was whiteness, and not nationality or religion or cultural heritage, that allowed access to the middle class. This also helped to form a sense of whiteness, a culture of belonging, in homogenous white communities that had been previously segregated by ethnicity.

Further, these segregated spaces prevented many white people from ever having meaningful contact with people of color, or to hear about and begin to trust their experiences with racism and discrimination. In this way, most whites failed to understand why it took more than hard work to attain the middle class, or at least stably working-class, status that many of them enjoyed. It was therefore "common sense" to many whites that all one had to do was work hard, go to school, and get a decent job in order to be successful. Overt racism was therefore unnecessary; one could simply believe that some people lacked the will or role models to do these things, while others, like them, could and did. Whites were not blocked from owning property, could benefit from intergenerational transfers of wealth, and lived in places where property taxes supported quality public schools that became vehicles for further success. And they could do all of this no matter their individual level of prejudice.

This is perhaps further complicated by the fact that these New Deal reforms made at least some inroads for black Americans, who tended to eagerly support these Democratic policies for the minimal new protections and opportunities that they offered. "The Democratic Party mobilized blacks in two distinct phases, each of which reflected the centrality of white voters to their political strategy and the secondary status of black voters" (de Leon 2011: 87). From 1932–65 this took place largely through symbolic gestures, with few meaningful transformations in policy that would further open doors of opportunity and access to the securities and protections that they afforded. As de Leon also writes, "The New Deal voting bloc therefore comprised the political incarnation of colorblind ideology, within which black juridical rights were permissible so long as white privileges in key redistributive programs remained untouched" (2011: 88). These tensions would prove invaluable to the resistance that came along next during the Civil Rights Movement. They would also have an impact upon the negotiation of southern politics, in particular, around blacks and whites as voting publics.

From Freedom to Civil Rights

This evolution from, roughly, overt into covert racism also mirrors the way that the Civil Rights Movement has been understood. This is also reflected in the language used to describe it in contemporary political and even scholarly discourse. What we now call the Civil Rights Movement of the 1950s and 1960s was first called the Freedom Movement. The language of the "Civil Rights Movement" rather than the Freedom Movement began to gain traction in the 1950s and was in widespread use in the 1960s (Lawson 2011: 24). Similarly, what we now call only the "March on Washington" where King gave his famous "I Have a Dream" speech in 1963 was in fact the "March on Washington for Jobs and Freedom." Dominant discourse, indeed, has a curious way of truncating this element of the movement's history, much as King's "I Have a Dream" speech, so familiar for its refrains around prejudice in the last third of the speech, focuses in the first two-thirds on jobs, housing, police brutality, segregation, and other elements of structural racism and violence. As such, through the elements of this famous speech that we tend to emphasize, and through the names given to the movement and its major rallies, we also support language that is colorblind rather than more sharply critical of institutional racism.

The movement's history has also been sanitized and made reflective of the status quo that has in many ways subsumed it. Black women were key organizers in this movement: fighting to prosecute white men who committed sexual assault against them, standing up for their status as wives of veterans and workers, and acting as central leaders in the religious and civic communities that were vital in mobilizing resistance. Similarly, very few people know that it was a gay black man, Bayard Rustin, who organized the 1963 March on Washington for Jobs and Freedom. The movement was in fact a multi-faceted coalition, with some organizations and efforts focusing on "black–red" alliances around social class or anti-imperialism. The fact that so few of these more radical strains of the Freedom Movement are widely known likely reflects "the New Right's efforts to reinterpret the classic Civil Rights Movement exclusively as an attempt to obtain individual opportunity on a colorblind basis, mainly through the right to vote, without challenging the economic or political system" itself (Lawson 2011: 13).

At the same time, as Nancy MacLean (2008) points out in her book of the same name, freedom is not enough. Drawing on Lyndon Johnson's 1965 commencement address at Howard University, her book details the struggle for access to quality jobs as a core element of the struggle for freedom. She writes, "in challenging economic exclusion as a denial of full and fair citizenship, African Americans began a process that shifted the very axis of the United States" (4). While her analysis is somewhat rosy in its celebration of diversity in the US workforce, her historical emphasis on the activism of people of color and women in pushing for these forms of freedom are central to understanding the Civil Rights struggles of the 1960s. "Nearly every movement for equality since then has followed the black struggle in concluding that legal freedom, formal equality, was not enough. Rather, genuine inclusion – full belonging as Americans – required participation in the economic mainstream – namely, access to good jobs at all levels once reserved for white men alone" (5). This lack of emphasis on structural inequalities reflects the larger color-blind practice of sanitizing the Civil Rights Movement into one of changing attitudes rather than changing policies.

A similar strategy was used in efforts that focused on voting, even as it manifested in less radical forms:

> Without question, liberals pursued a far more restrained economic agenda, but they continued to link antiracism with economic reform. Their emphasis on the expansion of the constitutional right to vote was not an exercise in abstract legalism; it offered a strategy to boost black voting power and thus enhance efforts to extend minimum wage, full employment, and social security legislation; provide public housing; and repeal the antiunion Taft-Hartley Act. (Lawson 2011: 18)

The success of these measures are perhaps reflected in recent efforts to dismantle core elements of the Voting Rights Act, which most political analysts agree will have the clear effect of disenfranchising large numbers of black voters. Similar longstanding efforts to gerrymander voting districts seem to have the same effect: "Gerrymandering, as it is called, is a very old practice used historically by whites to ensure white-majority voting control over a district or municipality" (Darling 2001: xix).

And so, while the Civil Rights Movement represented an incredible success in guaranteeing legal protections against overt forms of discrimination, it is crucial to remember that ongoing subtle, or *de jure*, forms of racism are not only still in operation, but are also entirely legal. Family wealth continues to grow unequally by race. Discrimination persists through implicit biases. Our schools are still vastly unequal, their funding coming from neighborhoods that remain segregated by these histories of unequal access to education, wealth, and employment. This should not mean that we write off the Freedom Movement for the crucial steps that it made to overcome the Jim Crow system of racial exclusion. As McAdam (1999) writes, "That the movement failed to eliminate the last vestiges of racial discrimination in this country is undeniable, but the failure is hardly proof of the ineffectiveness of the 'politics of protest.' Instead, the persistence of discrimination attests to the combined power of the forces arrayed against the sorts of fundamental systemic changes that would be required to eliminate institutional racism" (232). And, of course, the struggle for freedom has continued in the decades since.

Cold War Politics and Neoliberal Racism

The post-Civil Rights era, where most have suggested the evolution into colorblind racism most firmly took hold, is also characterized by the decades of Cold War politics and, especially, the global evolution into neoliberal politics and economic systems. Colorblindness is deeply complicit with neoliberal ideology, for both assert the centrality of individual actors who are unfettered by either oppressive social systems, from which they can rise above through the use of hard work and competition; or systems of governmental support, which are thought to suppress rather than support this meritocratic system. This way of thinking was particularly appealing to growing numbers of white Americans, who toward the end of the Civil Rights Movement "rallied around a 'color-blind' discourse of suburban innocence that depicted residential segregation as the class-based outcome of merito-cratic individualism rather than the unconstitutional product of structural racism" (Lassiter 2006: 1).

Beginning with the 1968 election, in what is often referred to as the Southern Strategy, there emerged a strong "rights-based discourse peppered with allusions to liberty, freedom, and individual autonomy" (de Leon 2011: 89). Tapping Southern resistance to the Civil Rights efforts around desegregation, Republican strategists began to target suburban white voters who were concerned about the impact of integration on their neighborhoods and schools. The Southern Strategy therefore "refers to an effort to gain political support for conservative Republican candidates; appealing to oftentimes coded but sometimes overt, racist messages directed at disaffected whites" (Inwood 2015: 408). In this way, "… opponents of busing describe the government as dictating, telling, making, and inflicting. Indeed, the emergent discourse is profoundly one of white victimization, innocence, and entitlement" (ibid.).

This is perhaps nowhere more clear than in the words of key Republican strategist Lee Atwater, who said:

> The key is how abstract and how you handle the race thing. In other words, you start out, you start out in 1954 by saying 'nigger, nigger, nigger,' [but] by 1968 you can't say nigger, that hurts you, backfires, so you say stuff like 'forced bussing,' 'states rights,' and all that stuff. At this point, you're getting so abstract now, you're talking about cutting taxes, by this time you're talking about all these economic things, and the by-product of them is, blacks get hurt worse than whites. What I am saying is, that if it is getting this abstract, and that coded, then we're doing away with the racial problem, because obviously sitting around saying, we want to cut taxes, is much more abstract than even the bussing thing, and a hell of a lot more abstract than 'nigger, nigger.' (Inwood 2015: 415)

This jarring and often-cited passage is a perfect representation of what Bonilla-Silva (2003) would later indeed call
the *abstract* liberalism frame: "using the ideas associated
with political liberalism ... and economic liberalism ... in an
abstract matter to explain racial matters" (28).

Inwood (2015), in his exploration of the Southern Strategy,
draws on the work of David Harvey, who writes that "'an
open project around the restoration of economic power to a
small elite would probably not gain much popular support"
so what was needed was an appeal based on "traditional and
cultural values" (Inwood 2015: 40). "There is not a more
traditional cultural value in the USA than white supremacy
and white privilege" (418). Schooling issues, for example,
were a central way to recruit white parents into Republican
party politics, and away from possible ongoing support for
movements for racial equality. These whites, often suburban,
were skeptical of integration – racial fears that were easily
tapped by the growing power of the right. "Richard Nixon
called suburban families the Forgotten Americans, and then
the Silent Majority, and finally the New American Majority"
(Lassiter 2006: 5). But this shift in support was not limited
to suburban white voters. Support for Democratic candidates among union voters dropped by half from 1964 to
1968 (Frymer 2008: 3).

The right was eager to capture votes and play on racial
anxieties of white Americans. Such pandering is exemplified in
comments like Ronald Reagan's in 1984: "They favor busing
that takes innocent children out of the neighborhood schools
and makes them pawns in a social experiment that nobody
wants" (cited in F. Brown 2004: 192). Even so, this understanding of the Southern Strategy is not without its critics.

> The widespread tendency to attribute the conservative shift
> in American politics to a top-down "Southern Strategy,"
> launched by the Republican party in order to exploit white
> backlash against the Civil Rights movement, misses the longer-
> term convergence of southern and national politics around the
> suburban ethos of middle-class entitlement. (Lassiter 2006: 3)

Crespino (2007) also cautions that we should consider changes in the South's economy in these same years, complicating the role of Southern elites in marshaling a number of co-evolving policies. He also emphasizes that "conservative color blindness and racist code words were not the invention of Republican presidential strategists or of white suburbanites. They had always been a part of segregationist politics in [the] Deep South" (8).

Still, they were successful. Reagan took an obsessive interest in both welfare and crime, to which he tagged pervasive racial imagery. As Alexander (2010) writes, "At the time [Reagan] declared this new war [on drugs], less than two percent of the American public viewed drugs as being the most important issue facing the nation. This fact was no deterrent to Reagan, for the drug war from the outset had little to do with public concern about drugs and much to do with public concerns about race" (49). Using this colorblind, neoliberal framework about fairness, safety, and "law and order," Reagan built on the conservative movement's efforts to capture the racial resentments of whites. And, as many others have pointed out, Reagan also used these strategies to fund and defend a "war on drugs," which has had a devastating impact on black and brown communities, who are disproportionally policed, despite comparable if not lower rates of drug use (see Alexander 2010). Reagan also invented the trope of the welfare queen, a pervasive but mythical racialized controlling image, which has also had a strong impact on many voters' willingness to support public aid (see Quadagno 1994). Indeed, this divestment in "entitlement programs" continued under President Obama, who boasted about $650 billion in cuts to these programs (George 2013: 241).

Obama's presidency, of course, was meaningful for many from across the political spectrum. In the end, his politics favored neoliberalism (George 2013) by advancing policies that supported privatization and diminished social services spending. He also proved to be no less colorblind than his predecessors – only occasionally discussing the realities of racism and instead focusing on our shared values and experiences. When he did discuss the realities of racism, as in his speech in response to his former pastor Jeremiah Wright's sermons "damning" the United States for its racism, he tended to emphasize the point that tremendous progress had been made. As de Leon (2011) writes,

> The internal dynamics of the Obama campaign, to the extent that they have been reported, confirm that the organization was doing what so many Democratic campaigns had done before it, namely court white voters above all while doing just enough to guarantee the black vote. (94)

Bonilla-Silva and Dietrich (2011) have similarly traced Obama's use of colorblind rhetoric, and argue that his use thereof has been central to his success. That the Trump presidency followed as both a resurgence of white power and a continuation of colorblind, neoliberal politics in the United States should perhaps come as no surprise. As such, sociological and most other social scientific consensus holds that we are far from the "post-racial" America that the early hopes of Obama's presidency held for many in the mainstream.

Discussion Questions

- To what extent has the history you've learned been colorblind?
- What was your prior perception of the Civil Rights Movement – both its areas of focus, and how much it was able to achieve?
- To what extent do current political parties/movements use colorblind, coded, or white supremacist language? How do you think that impacts upon their voting base?

Study of Racism in the Social Sciences

It is also important to recognize how deeply the US history explored above, and the intellectual and scientific discourse that surrounds it, are intertwined. As sociologist Dorothy Smith points out, "knowledge of society must always be from a position in it" (2005: 8); everything that we know, either through empirical or theoretical examination, is generated from within the same social world that we want to explore. As such, it will be always be in some way influenced by the society that surrounds it. This is certainly true for society's racial ideologies, whether they are explicitly white supremacist or colorblind. As the historical section above demonstrated, colorblindness is not confined to only recent decades. Racism was pervasive but rarely couched solely as such. This was no less true in scholarship that attempted to study it. In fact, as Bonilla-Silva (1997) points out, the term "racism" was not used in American sociology until 1945! Obviously racism was deeply entrenched in American life prior to that time, and so it was not that racism only emerged for social scientists to study at that time. Rather, this reality reflects the ways that scholars of color were marginalized and how white scholars', mostly men's, own experiences with the world shaped the way that they studied and theorized about it. If racism was not a problem for them, it was not seen as a significant social problem. Sociology was not the only academic discipline infected by these biases, and has since emerged among the leading disciplines sharply focusing attention on the realities of racism today. For this reason, a brief examination of its history in both reflecting and then analyzing both racist and colorblind ideologies helps us to further understand the relationship between racial ideologies and larger social practices.

White Supremacy and Eugenics

While the earliest days of colonial settlement in what was becoming the United States used other lenses, such as land ownership and religion, for categories of identity and practices of power, the idea of race soon emerged to further clarify and cement those hierarchies. It did so by creating a new category called whiteness, in order to assert and justify race-based domination. Indeed, the word "white" was first used in policy in 1790 in order to carve boundaries around an elite group of Anglo-Saxon Protestants, who in the USA's first immigration act were then declared eligible for citizenship as "free white persons." This important phrase not only began to create these boundaries around whiteness as a category of privilege and protection, but also further institutionalized slavery, which was made permanent and inheritable for black people, and indentured servitude as a temporary condition for poor whites. The phrase also resolved, for a time, the tension between the claim in the Declaration of Independence that "all men are created equal," even as a number of the authors of this foundational legal document held human beings as property, fundamentally denying their freedom as men and women.

White supremacy was therefore created as a national project to defend such stark contradictions, with both natural sciences, in the form of eugenics, and social sciences mobilized to defend it. As Omi and Winant 2015) write, "Social science was shaped, not only by the European founding fathers, but also by the Social Darwinist currents of the period. As did virtually all the early figures, these [early founders of American sociology] adhered to the unquestioned white supremacy of their time" (5). Or, as Aldon Morris (2015) put it, "The racial analyses of white social scientists... provided ideological cover for racism" (3). This adherence took two forms. The most obvious were those now-discredited Social Darwinist practices that created hierarchies based on biased notions of culture that situated the cultures and societies of the industrializing West as models for civilization. They claimed, in short, that a process of "natural selection" and "survival of the fittest" applied to social systems in ways that mirror natural systems.

This, of course, was a neat fit to the biological notions of superiority that were fast developing in the natural sciences in order to defend slavery and the conquest of native lands. And it was a deep denial of the unequal systems of power that allow some to suffer and others to thrive. In fact, "the first American sociological journal, the *American Journal of Sociology*, founded by the Chicago sociologist Albion Small, exposed sociologists to ... eugenics" (Morris 2015: 19) in a lead article by European scientist Francis Galton, which was reprinted in the foundational sociology textbook *Introduction to the Science of Sociology* by Robert E. Park and Ernest Burgess (ibid.). This book also included work by Mississippi planter Alfred Stone, who argued that whites must assert control over disorderly populations of former slaves in order to resolve the "Negro Problem" (Magubane 2016: 381). In this sense early sociological scholarship was both overtly racist, in its support of white supremacist logics like eugenics, and also colorblind – emphasizing *cultural* traits to support Social Darwinism.

Marginalization of Black Scholars and the Chicago School of Sociology

The second and most pervasive practice in sociology, however, was even more colorblind, in that it ignored the topic of race and the realities of racism entirely, and instead focused on the problems and issues of white men and women – most often questions of social class. When women and gender issues were examined, it was those of upper-middle-class women's economic dependence on men, such as in the work of sociologist and novelist Charlotte Perkins Gilman – who herself abided by eugenics thinking. It was black scholars like W. E. B. DuBois and Anna Julia Cooper who articulated early studies of race and racism as non-biological and connected to systems of power, though they were marginalized in their time and for many of the decades that followed.

As Aldon D. Morris writes in his important reclamation of DuBois and his work, "There is an intriguing, well-kept secret regarding the founding of scientific sociology in America. The first school of scientific sociology in the United States was founded by a black professor located in a historically black university in the South. This reality flatly contradicts the accepted wisdom" (2015: 1). Morris went on to write:

> DuBois's sociological analyses, based on surveys, ethnographic research, massive interviews and participant observation, took him behind cultural stereotypes of the black masses, enabling him to realistically describe the conditions with which they struggled, conditions that were unknown to the [white] public and most social scientists. (2015: 42)

DuBois's contributions in *The Philadelphia Negro* were among the most systematic and rigorous of its time, and has even been called the first empirical sociological study (Morris 2015: 45). "Because he believed that an authentic social science was possible and that inferior and superior races did not exist, DuBois was the first social scientist to establish a sociological laboratory where systematic empirical research was conducted to determine the scientific causes of racial inequality" (Morris 2015: 3). The book made use of interviews with every single family in the neighborhood under study, as well as deep ethnographic study and extensive use of archival and other secondary materials. Morris writes, "Sociologists of the period usually ignored class distinctions among blacks, thus treating them as a homogenous mass. DuBois analyzed the black class structure and demonstrated how it shaped the community and its stratification dynamics" (2015: 47).

DuBois was also among the first to take what we now call an intersectional approach to his scholarship, devoting non-negligible attention to the specific ways that black women navigate racism and sexism from a place of structural marginalization. As Aldon Morris forgivingly suggests, "White scholars of the second half of the twentieth century did not purposely ignore DuBois; rather, thanks to the marginalization of DuBois by the white founders of sociology, they were ignorant of his work" (2015: xv). At the same time, as Mendenhall et al. (2017) note, "While this reframing of DuBois's scholarship is necessary, the erasure of black women's contributions to this rich scholarship needs to be addressed as well" (1231). Even DuBois, when citing Anna Julia Cooper, referred to her only as "a woman of the race" (Washington 1988).

Cooper, born the same year as the widely recognized sociologist Emile Durkheim, wrote *A Voice from the South* ([1892] 1988) as a systematic treatment of black American life as it relates to broader patterns in literature, history, art, feminism, and the struggle for black liberation. In doing so, she specifically situated black women as privileged knowers, uniquely poised to trace the interlocking systems of social inequalities that deeply shaped American life. Similarly, Ida Wells-Barnett, born just two years before Cooper, used her activist roots to create a sociology that begins in the standpoint of the oppressed to trace how interconnected social and ideological systems shape the realities that subordinated groups encounter in everyday life. The fact that these strains in the work of black women who were born to slaves seem so freshly modern reveals the degree to which sociology itself has been, and remains, shaped by power relations that suppress our ability to see the depth and breadth of the social systems that we claim to canvass "objectively." (Of course, the same is true for other social sciences and academic disciplines.)

It was only in the work of the much more widely recognized Chicago School of Sociology in the 1940s, which used ethnographic methods to study urban life, that scholars began

> to rework social scientific approaches to race, and eventually reinvented much of the wheel that DuBois had created two decades earlier ... . Just as black popular music – blues and jazz – could only gain popular currency when white musicians played it, black racial theory could only begin to make headway in the 'mainstream' social sciences when reframed and advanced by white scholars. (Omi and Winant 2015: 6)

Even so, the Chicago School scholars conceived of racism only in a more sanitized and power-neutral framework of "race relations." As Magubane (2016) writes, "The histories and strivings of African descent people can, therefore, be relegated to a space of their own, defined as 'race relations' or 'the sociology of race', which is itself set apart from 'general' sociology and its study of 'modernity'. Because of the way in which race is 'segregated as a "topic" within sociology', little room is left for discussion of how race has 'structured and continues to structure the sociological enterprise'" (370). This reflects the larger minimization of racism that undergirds colorblind racist ideologies and practices even today.

Marxist and Class-Centered Traditions

For much of the twentieth century, a focus on culture, including assimilationist models in the Chicago School comparing racial integration to immigrant integration, dominated sociological theories around race, most often tacitly blaming culture for a lack of success. This began to change with the work of Bob Blauner (1972), whose emphasis was centrally on exploitation and control, which he framed as colonial struggles, both reflective of and reproducing the larger project of extraction and expansion that are central to imperial nation-building. This shift toward structure rather than imagined deficiencies of culture was therefore important in theorizing about US racism. But this, too, can subvert efforts to understand fully the dynamics of racial inequality, particularly when the primary emphasis is placed on social class. The Marxist tradition is the most obvious of these trajectories, in its emphasis on labor-market conflicts and race or racism as a secondary method to divide the working class and assure the hegemony of the capitalist system. Slavery, in this context, is rightly understood as an engine of early capitalist production; at the same time, reducing slavery and its resultant racial hierarchies to class conflict and capitalist production misses the ways that logics of white supremacy permeate the social structure beyond class or relations of work. After all, as Bonilla-Silva (1997) writes, "even when class-based conflict becomes more salient in a social order, the racial component survives until the races' life chances are equalized and the mechanisms and social practices that produce those differences are eliminated" (471).

Contemporary class-centered analyses of race also can lend further credence to cultural explanations, as reflected in ongoing critiques of the work of William Julius Wilson. Wilson has written a number of books including *The Declining Significance of Race* (1980), *When Work Disappears* (1996), and *More Than Just Race* (2009) – the titles of which also reflect his emphasis on the centrality of economic forces to explain racial inequality. His work also emphasizes cultural responses to these structural, economic conditions, which has perpetuated a "culture of poverty" thesis that repeatedly fails the test of empirical or logical scrutiny. In contrast, Massey and Denton's *American Apartheid* (1993) refutes Wilson's emphasis on culture, exploring the deep and persistent hyper-segregation of American cities. They write, "our fundamental argument is that racial segregation – and its characteristic institutional form, the black ghetto – are the key structural factors responsible for the perpetuation of black poverty in the United States" (9). While an improvement over Wilson, these class-centered analyses still do not take into account how racism develops a life of its own and reaches into other spheres, even if it is in fact connected to strategies to preserve power among an elite economic class. In this way, such frameworks reflect colorblind ideologies, specifically the minimization of racism, rather than helping to scrutinize them.

Racial Ideologies and Racial Privilege

Michael Omi and Howard Winant's *Racial Formation in the United States*, first published in 1986 and now in its third edition (2015), was an attempt to reconcile competing frameworks and to help us understand the role of ideology in influencing racial outcomes, which are contested in concrete social locations. They write, "Our notion of racial formations foregrounds the ongoing political contestation that takes place between the state and civil society – across the political spectrum – to define and redefine the very meaning of race" (2015: 121). They focus specifically on racial projects, which "connect what race means in a particular discursive practice and the ways in which both social structure and everyday experiences are racially organized, based on that meaning" (125). While some have suggested that "the costs of being black and the benefits of being white do not figure in their theory. Racial formation is not analyzed in relation to racial advantage" (Wellman 1993: 9; for other critiques see Feagin and Elias 2013), their framework remains incredibly useful for understanding how racial inequality operates in discrete social settings where racist practices are justified according to prevailing ideological systems – colorblindness central among them. Omi and Winant, in their current edition of *Racial Formations*, write, "The hegemony of neoliberal economics is matched and underwritten by the racial hegemony of colorblindness" (2015: 211).

David Wellman's (1993) *Portraits of White Racism* also began to sharpen our focus on the defense of racial privilege in ways that echoed the emerging framework of colorblind racism. In his book, Wellman refers to the "contradiction confronting white Americans. The racial advantages they have traditionally enjoyed are threatened and they have few acceptable or legitimate options for defending them" (206). In this sense Wellman further conceptualized racism as a defense of racial privilege, both historically and now. In contemporary times, he identifies the common trend among whites, when confronted with the realities of racial inequality, to minimize racism, blame the victim, wax philosophical about opportunity, etc. These trends will sound familiar to readers of Eduardo Bonilla-Silva's (2003) *Racism without Racists*, which would first be published a decade later, for they mirror nearly verbatim Bonilla-Silva's frames, as well as the overarching theme of his book. Wellman writes, "Each position is formulated in very acceptable, almost liberal,

American terms. With some minor exceptions, there is not a prejudiced-sounding formulation among them" (208). That said, while Wellman's book took an important step toward, as did Omi and Winant's, recognizing the important role of ideology and discourse in defending social outcomes or "racial projects," it did not fully emphasize the social structures that must work in tandem with them in order to produce racism or unequal outcomes.

Racialized Social Systems and Systemic Racism

It was Eduardo Bonilla-Silva in 1997 who wrote a paradigm-shifting article called "Rethinking Racism: Toward a Structural Interpretation" in the *American Sociological Review*, one of sociology's top journals. Therein, Bonilla-Silva traced the flaws of prior models, where racism was not seen as central to the US social structure and had been reduced to individual attitudes. He writes, "if racism is not part of a society but is characteristic of individuals who are 'racist' or 'prejudiced' – that is, racism is a phenomenon operating at the individual level – then (1) social institutions cannot be racist and (2) studying racism is simply a matter of surveying the proportion of people in a society who hold 'racist' beliefs" (1997: 467). This echoes Frymer's comment that "Racism is not simply a matter that individuals must address with their therapists; rather, racism develops within a political context, and, as such, it is only through politics and collective struggle that we can confront it and reduce it" (2008: viii). Bonilla-Silva also pointed out how previous analyses of racism had treated it as static, irrational, overt, or a relic of the past, and had fallen prey to circular logics that did not allow us to meaningfully trace its prevalence in the entirety of our social systems.

Bonilla-Silva then proposed what he calls *racialized social systems* as a starting point for an alternative framework. This allows us to examine how, "in all racialized social systems the placement of people in racial categories involved some form of hierarchy that produces definite social relations between the races" (1997: 469). This produces tangible benefits and outcomes, which create the racial structure and hierarchies in a given society. He argues that "on the basis of this structure, there develops a racial ideology (what analysts have coded as racism). This ideology is not simply a 'superstructural' phenomenon (a mere reflection of the racialized social system), but becomes the organizational map that guides actions of racial actors in society. It becomes as real as the racial relations it organizes" (ibid.: 474). He also clarifies that racism is to be understood as an ideology "that crystallizes racial notions and stereotypes" (474). This further demarcates racism from individual expressions of bias, or the individual/psychological basis from which it had been studied in much prior scholarship.

It is also in some ways similar to Feagin's systemic racism approach, where "From a systemic racism perspective, US society is an organized racist whole with complex, interconnected, and interdependent social networks, organizations, and institutions that routinely imbed racial oppression" (Feagin [2006] 2013: 16). Feagin sees racism manifest in all institutions, foundational to United States history and persistent into the present. He also centers his analysis on the agency of whites in perpetuating this system, from which they reap considerable economic, social, and psychological benefits. *White-Washing Race: The Myth of a Color-Blind Society* (2003) by Brown et al. similarly details elements of this systemic racism, or in other words, why this color-blind society is a myth, but does not present a theoretical framework with which it can be understood. That same year, Bonilla-Silva published *Racism Without Racists: Color-Blind Racism and the Persistence of Racial Inequality in the United States*, which built upon his book two years prior, *White Supremacy and Racism in the Post-Civil Rights Era* (2001). *Racism Without Racists* fully brought into focus the connection between colorblindness and systemic understandings of racism, while advancing a concrete way to trace its central discursive frames. As discussed in the previous chapter, it has since set the paradigm for much research on contemporary racism in the decades that have followed.

Discussion Questions

- What are some ways that you have seen ideological systems impact upon ostensibly neutral scientific or theoretical frameworks?
- How does a focus on ideologies and social systems rather than individual prejudice change the way you might think and talk about racism?

Colorblindness and Growing Racial Inequality

Taken together, the historical threads of this chapter allow us to trace the paradox of growing contemporary racial inequality taking place after a movement, most actively in the 1960s, that worked to eradicate state-sanctioned segregation and discrimination. This also helps us understand the scholarship that has emerged around this paradox. From this, we can consider two important themes that may help us to better understand contemporary racism, and on that basis, how we might challenge it.

Pre-1960s Colorblindness

The first is in the fact that many pre-Civil Rights era laws and justifications that supported racial exclusion and segregation were not based on overt premises of racial hatred. This point has been emphasized by scholars like Cedric de Leon (see especially 2011): colorblind racism is not necessarily the "new" racism. As I have often told my students, policies like the Alien Land Acts, which restricted property ownership to whites in various Western states around the turn of the last century, was colorblind and abstract in *language* but vividly anti-Asian in its intentions and support. The same could be said for the 1924 Johnson–Reed Immigration Act, which took 1890 Census numbers and created evenly applied percentages of these numbers as national quotas. On the surface, this seems fair. Each nation was allowed equal percentages from this prior Census. However, there is a reason that 1890 was chosen for this 1924 law rather than the more-recent 1920 Census. By 1920, the nation's racial demographics had already begun to skew toward Southern and Eastern Europe, when immigrants from these nations were not yet considered white, and Asia. All of these populations were feared for their alleged inherent criminality and lack of intelligence. In 1890, the racial constitution of the United States was most heavily skewed toward Western Europe and "Anglo-Saxon Protestants," and was therefore much more desirable for the politics of white supremacy. And so, this colorblind law favored white supremacy. These are just two among many examples.

The history of the study of race and racism in the USA follows a similar logic; racism was minimized throughout much of this history of sociological and other social scientific scholarship as a result of the colorblind logic that travels with a white and male standpoint, from which the bulk of the influential scholarship has been and remains forged. The work of Zine Magubane (see 2016), Ruby Mendenhall, Brown, and Black (2017); and others is crucial in this regard. They allow us to see how writing out marginalized voices hurts our ability to trace more accurately the same social relations that sociologists and other social scientists are meant to study. While the field is slowly improving, these generations of erasure have dampened sociology's ability to trace this core feature of social life.

Ongoing Overt Racism

Another theme that is important to retain in the context of history in this chapter involves the ways that overt racisms persist even in the current "colorblind" era. And so, while the pre-Civil Rights eras were not exempt from colorblind logics and discourse, nor is the contemporary era free from "old-school," overt forms of racism. This was clear to many not only in some responses to Obama's campaign and presidency, but it has also been a consistent theme in research documenting both "race talk" (see Myers 2005) and other "back-stage" performances (Picca and Feagin 2007).

And so, while it is true that a defining characteristic of contemporary race relations in the post-Civil Rights era has been a decreased social acceptance of overt racism in most shared, and certainly public, spaces, neither racism nor its bold expression have waned. Instead, thanks to the work of previously (and still) marginalized scholars who have called our attention to its centrality in shaping social life, a sharpened focus on the abstracted, colorblind language and discourse in most institutional and social spaces has emerged. This dynamic is, of course, crucial to trace. The chapter that follows examines the wide array of scholarship that has allowed us to document the prevalence and impact of this framework. Even so, we must not lose sight of the persistence of racism that does not neatly follow this model. Some of that messier terrain is explored later in this book. Others are hiding, as they say, in plain sight.

Further Exploration

- Examine a historical text, either scholarly or popular, that is adjacent to or about racial issues. How is race and racism considered? Where can you detect colorblind frameworks and/or other racial ideologies?
- Challenge yourself to read deeply the work of Anna Julia Cooper, W. E. B. DuBois, or other marginalized scholars, to which most scholarship has been inattentive. How can you incorporate their insights into your next project?

3

Colorblindness in Divergent Contexts

To date, most of the research on colorblind racism has been devoted to documenting its presence, tracing how this ideology and especially its discursive frames show up in policy, institutions, culture, and our everyday lives. This is an important area for us to explore, as it helps us to appreciate just how far we are from the ideal of a society where race does not matter – even and perhaps especially when we try to act in accordance with those values. In all of the areas of life that this chapter will explore, we can see how pretending that race doesn't matter, in fact perpetuates racial inequality. This can happen when we apply law and policy without sensitivity to racial disparities. It can also happen when we pretend that we don't see race in our interactions with one another, as colorblindness is also deeply embedded in our culture. Most of the research helps us to reckon with these realities, improving our ability to understand how racism persists even after the successes of the Civil Rights Movement. It also helps us to see the urgent need to learn more about the workings of contemporary racism, so that we are best prepared to challenge it. Only in this way will we live up to the ideals of equality and freedom that so many of us cherish.

Colorblindness in Institutions

Perhaps the largest body of research on colorblind racism documents its existence inside institutions, often by demonstrating how colorblind principles have thwarted efforts toward racial equality. Colorblind ideologies are particularly pervasive in the institutional sites of education, housing, health care, and policing – which are then often reflected in policy. In some ways this makes sense: institutions and laws aim to create ideal worlds that are often in conflict with the individuals who navigate them. For example, we want to have a society where, to paraphrase the Reverend Dr. Martin Luther King, Jr., we are judged by the content of our character and not the color of our skin. The places where we go to school, live, receive medical care, and administer justice, *should* not be determined by one's race. But the reality remains that, despite our best intentions, they often are. Our schools and communities are deeply segregated; racial stereotypes continue to shape our interactions with one another; and the history explored in the last chapter continues to confer unearned advantages on many whites. In this way, these colorblind ideals can strangle the very process that they seek to ensure.

Education

This is perhaps nowhere more insidious than in the context of education. For example, research has shown how the emphasis on a "friendly" environment in suburban, mixed-race high schools has often also meant the evasion of any discussion about race, particularly given white anxieties about being labeled racist. This also leaves schools unable to address the very real racial tensions and inequities present within them. Marianne Modica, who studied this phenomenon, writes, "Silence about race denies students the skills they need to talk about race openly and honestly and the opportunity to think about how racism affects them and their relationships with others. Teachers who believe it is best to be colorblind lose the opportunity to address racial inequity in their classrooms and in their overall school programs" (2015: 397–8). Chapman's (2013) study, also of majority-white suburban schools, goes a step further to suggest that, in fact, this creates hostile learning environments for students of color at these schools, who are further disadvantaged when they discuss the realities of racism that negatively shape their experiences. They are seen as trouble-makers disrupting the pleasant environment of the school, rather than as a reflection of how unpleasant schools can be for students of color who regularly face bias, double standards, tracking, and other unfair treatment within them.

Such approaches to the realities of racism are characteristic of the approach to race in much of the US K-12 school system. Stoll (2013) suggests that despite their best intentions, too often teachers "are generally oblivious to the ways in which their words and behaviors reinforce dominant narratives about race and gender" (120). In particular, "the color- and gender-blind classroom is built on the assumption – indeed, the stated maxim – that every student can learn and be successful regardless of social location. It is a learning environment that welcomes the celebration of diversity while denying the existence of institutional racism and sexism" (123). Amy Brown (2013) has found that white teachers in urban public schools relied on narratives of colorblind meritocracy in ways that prevented them from being critical of neoliberal practices that both shape and exist within their schools. This is particularly vivid in Joseph et al.'s (2016) examination of the impact of colorblind ideology on black female adolescents in high schools, who experienced extreme racism and sexism from their majority white teachers. A study of teachers working with immigrant populations in Germany demonstrated that teachers with non-colorblind beliefs, who instead deliberately value cultural diversity, demonstrated better student outcomes than those with colorblind beliefs and pedagogical approaches (Hachfield et al. 2015). Despite promising findings like these, colorblind approaches, which ignore racial disparities and cultural differences, prevail – to the detriment of students.

Universities, despite their often more intentional focus on diversity and social justice, are often little better. White faculty mentoring students of color too often use a colorblind approach that also influences their perception of students of color as inferior and less interested in opportunities that lead to success (McCoy et al. 2015). When faculty do not appreciate how deeply racism shapes students' experiences, and how this may lead to more stress or divestment among students of color, they are of course inclined to blame the individual rather than the culture of a campus that has such a diminishing effect on students of color. When white students mock Asian students on their campus, or perpetually choose black students last for study groups and partners, students of color are bound to divest from these relationships and the opportunities that they can also provide.

Further, Harper (2012) has shown that even those who are interested in understanding these disparities on college campuses tend to deploy the minimization of racism frame in interpreting their results: "Rarely were racism and racist institutional norms explicitly named among the range of plausible reasons for racial differences" (16). This is despite the fact that students of color across the racial spectrum on predominantly white campuses tend to have negative experiences that are a direct result of white students' racial assumptions and deployment of colorblind ideologies (Lewis, Chesler, and Forman 2000), including the fact that "traditional racist talk is even more common than the race talk underlying the more subtle forms of racist oppression we associate with 'colorblind' racism" (Zamudio and Rios 2006: 485; see also Myers 2005). That is, it is still not at all uncommon for university students to use the N-word or scrawl it in public spaces, to host parties where people of color's bodies and assumed cultures are mockingly used as costumes, or to effectively lock students of color out of social spaces and clubs.

There have been some efforts to mitigate this, and to work intentionally with white students in order to improve the experiences of students of color. This is the explicit goal in a pre-orientation program that I developed with Kira Banks, a psychology colleague who first approached me with the idea. Our program is designed to enhance the competence and confidence for white students to challenge racism and partner in racial and social justice efforts on campus. They do this by scrutinizing colorblind ideology and developing an intersectional awareness of their white privilege. In short, they work on *themselves* in order to be prepared to support their classmates, and one another, in improving the campus climate around race. Our program has demonstrated a significant decrease in colorblind racial ideology (Burke and Banks 2012), which continued to hold under longitudinal testing (Banales 2014). Jayakumar (2015) has looked more broadly at the lasting impact of the college experience on whites' colorblind racial attitudes, after all, and found that white students from homogenous racial backgrounds tend to uphold or return to colorblind frameworks post-college, unless they have had significant experiences with diversity in their curriculum or experiences while on campus. Even so, most white students remain immersed in their white habitus, which maintains both physical and mental segregation from people of color, while on campus, much as they do before and after.

These realities also extend to the experiences of black student athletes (Bimper 2015), and are found even when multicultural education is an explicit goal. This is because, often, too few curricular connections are made to structural and institutional inequalities and the ongoing privileging of whiteness, especially under the framework of meritocracy (Castagno 2013). Patton (2004) has similarly suggested that "sexism and racism in higher education have been allowed to continue in the guise of civility" (62), all while "the interests of certain races, classes, genders, and sexualities are valued over the interests of others" (67) at the institutional level. As Zamudio and Rios (2006) note, "it is our position that any university's silence on issues of racism allows the attitudes and actions of white students ... to take root and thrive on campus" (499). Universities simply must do better to be intentional about talking about race and racism, mitigating racism's effects, and in sharing the load in educating all students about the realities of the world that they will soon encounter as working adults.

Workplaces and Health Care

This is all the more important, because the same dynamics often shape workplace experiences. As Jensen et al. note, much like in schools, "diversity approaches [in the workplace] reflect the organizations' normative beliefs and expectations about the reason to diversify, the value of cultural diversity, and its connection to work processes" (2016: 81). They found that Dutch non-Western minority employees found greater job satisfaction when they perceived multicultural rather than colorblind approaches in their workplaces – that is, where cultural differences were acknowledged and valued, and this was reflected in leadership and representation. This is reflective of larger debates around diversity in the workforce, and how it has too often been co-opted. Embrick (2011) argues, based on a study with upper-level managers in *Fortune 1000* companies, that "diversity ideology has enabled many organizations to curtail deeper investigations into the gender and racial inequalities that continue to persist in the workplace" (542). In short, proclaiming the value of diversity seems *alone* to stand in for any meaningful efforts to produce or maintain diversity or equality in their workforce, especially by excluding race and gender from their conceptions of diversity. This is the hallmark of a colorblind and gender-blind approach to diversity broadly, and to workplace equity in particular. As Embrick explains, "By increasing the number of categories of people that fall under the umbrella of diversity, companies are able to effectively escape close examination of racial and gender inequalities that might occur in their workplaces. As long as no one brings it up, it can be ignored" (2011: 547).

This racial logic also extends to health-care institutions. Malat et al. (2010) interviewed white doctors and nurses about their perceptions of racial inequality in the US health-care system, and found that even when they acknowledged mechanisms that provide whites with better care than people of color, they still upheld a colorblind approach and avoided implicating themselves in these same systems that they discussed with such familiarity. In particular, they blamed black patients' assumed behaviors (such as not complying with doctors' recommendations) for disparate outcomes, and attributed whites' access to care to their proactive approach to heath care. They acknowledged the bias that is present in the system, but refused to see this as a primary factor in the inequities produced by this system. This in part demonstrates the flexibility of colorblind ideology, a topic to which we will turn in Chapter 4, but also how deeply it is entrenched in the very institutions that have a direct impact on the health and well being of individuals who are embedded in them.

Criminal Justice

This is perhaps nowhere more stark than in the criminal justice system, where racial bias has been documented at every stage of the potential process, from first contact with police officers to sentencing of life and death thereafter. Indeed, colorblindness is a central theoretical framework of Michelle Alexander's (2010) book *The New Jim Crow*, where she traces how a new caste system of mass incarceration has replaced the more overt and formal systems of racial oppression with a new discourse of criminality. She writes:

> In the era of colorblindness, it is no longer socially permissible to use race, explicitly, as a justification for discrimination, exclusion, and social contempt. So we don't. Rather than rely on race, we use our criminal justice system to label people of color 'criminals' and then engage in all the practices we supposedly left behind. Today it is perfectly legal to discriminate against criminals in nearly all the ways that it was once legal to discriminate against African Americans. (2)

Her book goes on to detail discrimination in housing, voting, schooling, employment, welfare access, jury service, and a myriad of other settings. It also carefully traces the process by which the presumption of guilt, strongly driven by racial bias that is also well documented, can steer *innocent* poor black and brown people into the system, given the legal costs and other barriers that make it difficult to prove one's innocence. As such, even those who have committed no crime can be trapped by the debt, stigma, and formal exclusions that can follow a guilty verdict or, more often, a plea bargain.

Alexander's book contains a wealth of resources detailing the racial biases and consequences of such a system, despite black and brown folks being no more likely to sell, deal, or traffic in drugs, which are the most frequent of the charges that bring people into the system. But some further studies are still worth our consideration for detailing how we allow such stark inequalities to persist. Sharla Alegria (2012) conducted focus group research with white Americans about documented racial profiling by police officers. She found that participants made active but often coded use of racial stereotypes, and justified stops of black people by police in white neighborhoods "because they are 'out of place', which is not a crime. Participants expected police to suspect white people in black neighborhoods of possessing drugs. In other words, white people who associate with black people are accountable for behaviors expected from black people" (256).

This reveals just some of the ways that whites, whose lives are not ravaged by the deep-seated biases in the criminal justice system and its lifelong consequences, rationalize this system and therefore continue to accept it. A similar dynamic takes place in broad support for, or indifference to, ostensibly race-neutral sentencing laws that disproportion-ately affect blacks. After all, as Gonzalez Van Cleve writes, "through these 'colorblind lenses' that dismiss the continued role of racial discrimination, racially disparate incarceration is often interpreted as an indicator of the alleged cultural dysfunction or immorality of people of color" (Van Cleve and Maze 2015: 407). Schlesinger (2011) makes a similar point: "This system allows white people to believe in the justice of the criminal justice system. Once they believe the system is just, the fact of racial disparity in imprisonment will reinforce whites' beliefs in the (either genetic or cultural) criminality of black people" (74).

Neighborhoods and Communities

Sadly, it is not only indifference or hostility that can justify disparate outcomes. My own research (Burke 2012a) has examined the tensions in racially diverse Chicago communities between their often-stated celebration of diversity and their deeply racialized concerns about safety and property values. In particular, I find that the "happy talk" (Bell and Hartmann 2007) around diversity quickly fades into ambivalence or outright refusal once it moves from the abstract land of discourse and into the real choices and activities embedded inside these neighborhoods (Burke 2012b). Mayorga-Gallo's (2016) findings were nearly identical in her study of Durham, North Carolina. Both of our books describe the existence of a white habitus, which is "a racialized, uninterrupted socialization process that conditions and creates whites' racial taste, perceptions, feelings, and emotions and their views on racial matters" (Bonilla-Silva, 2003: 104). It also preserves privileges for whites inside these racially diverse neighborhoods. As Mayorga-Gallo writes, "Even though various racial–ethnic communities live in the neighborhood, it is still a space that is primarily framed by the needs and desires of White residents, particularly, white homeowners" (2016: 149). We both also detail how whites consider diversity as a commodity, something that adds interest to their lives and that becomes important to their identity work as tolerant and unique individuals. They do this while actively policing the bodies of people of color, who continue to be considered "out of place" (Harris Combs 2016) in their neighborhoods, and putting their own self-interest ahead of the needs of their neighbors and community.

Dylan Gottlieb (2013) traced a similar kind of "white-washing" in the history of Zephyrhills, Florida, in the debates that surrounded a proposal to rename a city street for Martin Luther King, Jr. As Gottlieb notes, "the largely white constituency that opposed the name change framed the renaming as an affront to their personal rights as private citizens" (1086). They did this by either utilizing racial codes to make race-centered arguments against the renaming process, or by remaining genuinely naive about the racial politics that surround such debates. Such a debate, ironically, also then fostered a debate over the relevance of race in a community divided over a racial matter. As he writes, "White residents in Zephyrhills would not and could not use the language of race, even when discussing an issue that was impossible to understand apart from its racial dimension. Their commitment to colorblindness, well intentioned or not, pushed them to erase race from public discourse. Yet, simultaneously, they reaffirmed its relevance by using it to divide the community and silence African American self-representations" (1088).

Even well-established race scholars can reflect an ambivalence on the significance of race and place in a colorblind fashion. Elijah Anderson (2011) does so in his discussion of what he calls cosmopolitan canopies – urban spaces where "racially, ethnically, and socially diverse peoples spend casual and purposeful time together, coming to know one another through what [he calls] folk ethnography, a form of people watching that allows individuals informally to gather evidence in social interactions that supports their own viewpoints or transforms their common-sense under-standings of social life" (xv). And yet, as Anderson details, these spaces are still infused with racialized assumptions that disparately impact on those within them. As I wrote in my critique of Anderson relative to my findings in a diverse Chicago community:

> Living in a diverse community, enjoying and celebrating that diversity, identifying with liberal or progressive politics,

stumping for Obama, or shopping and eating [in] immigrant communities does not mean that one develops a race cognizance, the ability to navigate outside of the very narrow confines of color-blindness that have dominated the political discourse in the United States in the post-Civil Rights era. And it is these realities, taken in tandem, which have thus far created racially diverse communities that reproduce rather than democratize a white habitus, white wealth, and white privileges inside of otherwise diverse spaces. (Burke 2012a: 158–9)

It cannot be the mere presence of diversity, especially when it is there to be anonymously consumed, that creates true racial justice. We can be just as colorblind and racist, or at the very least participate in activities that uphold racial hierarchies, even when we "enjoy" diversity – and especially when we merely "tolerate" its presence. After all, who likes being tolerated?

Discussion Questions

• In what ways do the institutions and communities that surround you reflect colorblind ideologies and discourses around race?
• How might positive or "tolerant" discourse still be problematic in our institutions and communities?
• What are some ways that these institutions could change their policies to better support racial equality?

Colorblindness in Law and Policy

Even given the fact that tolerance is not alone ideal, as Martin Luther King, Jr. said in an address to Cornell College students in 1962, "It may be true that the law cannot make a man love me, but it can keep him from lynching me, and I think that's pretty important." This section will help us to understand how policy formalizes the covert nature of colorblindness discussed above by writing it into law and other formal processes. This is present not only in the US Constitution and an analysis of how it has been unevenly applied, but also in its impact on employment, admissions, immigration, housing, education, and welfare policies. In short, most law and policy tends to focus on the ideal of race-neutrality, while ignoring the current and historical dimensions that have actively used race to determine merit and administer opportunities and resources. As such, it presents the deepest exploration of the paradox that the very phrase "colorblind racism" embodies: it traces the basis for an uneven application of law under ostensibly equal premises.

Legal Studies

In many ways, the work done by legal scholars in the area of critical race theory (sometimes abbreviated as CRT) has provided the foundation for any examination of policy under the rubric of colorblindness. Legal scholar Kimberlé Crenshaw is credited with founding this area of study, which explores "the historical centrality and complicity of law in upholding white supremacy (and concomitant hierarchies of gender, class, and sexual orientation)" (West 1995: xi). Crenshaw's (1991) article "Mapping the Margins: Intersectionality, Identity Politics, and Violence Against Women of Color" explores the harmful consequences of conceptualizing women of color's experiences with violence as structured by either race *or* gender rather than appreciating how they are mutually constitutive. Importantly, she details how "intervention strategies based solely on the experiences of women who do not share the same class or race backgrounds will be of limited help to women who because of race and class face different obstacles" (1246).

This underlines the failure, as Crenshaw has argued elsewhere, of "a rhetorical strategy of transcendence to justify [court cases'] modern construction of colorblindness as a constitutional restriction on the state's use of racial classifications *even in its attempts to empower people of color* and investigate how this strategy protects white privilege" [emphasis in original] (1998: 244). Indeed, she argues, "colorblind discourse is becoming the primary vehicle for sanctioning appropriate legal and cultural 'race' relations" (245). These relations, of course, are reflective of, because they are created by, the power relations that crystalize racial hierarchies and privileges for whites. Again borrowing on Schlesinger's (2011) examination of sentencing policies and their disparate racial impact, "when racial disparity is produced through race-neutral policies, the institutionalization of racial difference is disguised" (74).

This happens because, as Boddie (2015) writes, "although it is the dominant paradigm in equal protection, colorblind individualism bears little resemblance to the lived experiences of race. Within the colorblind individualist framework, race-conscious selection policies presumptively violate equal protection because they place the racial group above the individual" (781). She goes on to argue that race-intentional policies and practices, when used to build a critical mass of underrepresented groups in an institutional space such as higher education, "can *reduce* the salience of race" (782, emphasis in original) – making members of those underrepresented groups less likely to be received as tokens but rather as individuals.

Further, Gotanda (1995) argues that the US Constitution, ostensibly a race-neutral document referring only to "persons," cannot be considered a colorblind document, for "a colorblind interpretation of the Constitution legitimates and thereby maintains the social, economic, and political advantages that whites hold over other Americans" (257). He suggests that while the US Supreme Court, in interpreting the Constitution, has used categories and language of race, it has done so without understanding or preventing its complicity in perpetuating racism. The large body of work in critical race theory, the surface of which is only lightly scratched here, provides an important foundation for understanding the ways in which laws and policies, despite universal intent, are forever particular when applied to real lives and contexts that are already structured by racial inequality.

Immigration Policy

US immigration policy represents a useful example of this phenomenon. Historically, race was central to determinations of citizenship, such as the 1790 Act that restricted naturalization to "free white persons" – deliberately leaving out slaves and other marginalized groups. The United States also passed the 1882 Chinese Exclusion Act, the first and only immigration policy deliberately singling out a national group based on deep hostility prompted by an economic recession and pervasive racist images and stereotypes of Chinese as violent and barbaric. At the same time, these overt examples of racial exclusion were coupled with early expressions of colorblind policy that still carried race-specific intent. The Alien Land Acts, for example, were designed to disenfranchise Asians in the Western states where they were written and applied, despite race neutrality in their language. The same can be said for the 1924 Hart–Cellar Immigration Act, which used national quotas from the 1880 Census to limit immigration in favor of Western Europeans until 1965. This Act did so without explicitly naming this racial preference, which was structured by racial hostility and eugenics thinking, in its theoretically race-neutral national quotas.

However, despite the 1965 Immigration Act's intention to remove these racially driven national quotas, the role of race in shaping responses to, and application of, those policies has not diminished. Instead, Douglas et al. demonstrate how "the principles of abstract liberalism and cultural racism emphasizing fairness, equality, and unassimilability have been used in the creation and marginalization of people of color as both undesired and unqualified for US citizenship" (2015: 1447). This has especially impacted Mexicans and other Latinx immigrants as well as those racialized as Muslim or Middle Eastern, who are disproportionately detained and deported in response to racialized rhetoric around safety and jobs. (For an accessible resource that unsettles these and other often-racialized myths around immigration see

Chomsky 2007.) President Trump's proposed travel bans on immigrants from predominantly Muslim countries, while contested in courts, uses religion and nation as a proxy for terrorism in ways that continue to racialize Muslims (Selod 2015). It is colorblind and yet deeply racially coded.

Education and Housing Policy

Education policy has also been strongly influenced by color-blind ideology. Freeman (2005) argues that "the selective and mechanistic policy approach followed by [No Child Left Behind, a national educational initiative created in 2001 by President George W. Bush] is synchronous with an ideology of colorblindness because it relies on the notion that numerical gains in academic performance are sufficient to dissolve the raft of social encumbrances incurred by children in the course of their everyday lives" (194). Importantly, he also suggests that this policy presents the illusion of progress, given that it purports to mediate social and racial inequalities that are deeply seated in the educational system but does not remedy the structural inequities that shape the school system or the outcomes for students upon graduation. He writes, "the hope that schools can rectify inequality through the provision of increased achievement and upward mobility has the virtue of promising justice with a minimum of pain and social dislocation" (197).

Similar dynamics shape housing policy. Anderson (2004) has explored how housing policy works "to prevent meaningful ways for public housing authorities to use race-neutral means to overcome their past role in maintaining and enforcing racial segregation" (846). She explores how the mandate that any proposed remedies for unconstitutional segregation and discrimination in housing should remain race-neutral actually serves to uphold racial inequalities in housing. While the 1968 Fair Housing Act made it illegal for barriers to entry to be determined by race, it is not alone able to remedy the structures of wealth and exclusion that, in effect, still bar disadvantaged families from gaining access to quality, safe housing. This is nowhere more clear than in public housing policies, where public health crises like lead poisoning and other elements of disrepair make for precarious living for its residents, who largely remain in racially segregated communities (see Desmond 2016). Instead, Michelle Anderson argues that "the harms wrought by segregation obligate courts to remedy the state role in administering segregation by unraveling its lasting effects" (2004: 847). However, the colorblind notion that any race-specific remedies constitute injustice has prevented steps like this from becoming a reality.

Affirmative Action and Welfare Policy

Other efforts at remediation, such as affirmative action policy, have been structured by similar dynamics. Affirmative action is widely misunderstood as being a policy that gives racial preferences to people of color. Instead, it seeks to deliberately create equal opportunity by ensuring that, for example, positions in jobs and schools are made available to qualified applicants from diverse settings, and that bias does not intervene in the process to prevent worthy candidates from being considered. Racial quotas, which many assume to be in place, have been illegal since 1978. Further, neither companies nor schools have any incentive (financial or otherwise) to hire or admit people who do not meet, and in reality far exceed, minimum requirements. Otherwise, companies would suffer from a less competitive workforce and schools could slip in rankings. The same is true for scholarship funds, which almost never have racial restrictions.

Berry and Bonilla-Silva (2008) explored how whites' exclusionary racial views are crystallized in their responses to affirmative action hiring scenarios and found that whites remain hesitant to support policies that they perceive to give preference to blacks, and adhere instead to colorblind notions about individual merit. López (2007) traces an "anticlassification understanding of the Equal Protection Clause that accords race-conscious remedies and racial subjugation the same level of constitutional hostility" (988) as overt segregation practices like Jim Crow. He argues that in attention to context in legal cases, it is clear that colorblindness has devolved from a progressive vision to a regressive way to defend the status quo. Indeed, a fellow legal scholar Bridgette Baldwin laments that "the language on race is so neutral that it has allowed whites to argue that racial preferences constitute reverse discrimination under the law" (2009: 866), despite a lack of evidence of legal exclusion based on their race. She further argues that this removes prior affirmative action court decisions (e.g. *Bakke* – which made quotas illegal) from their original contexts.

Perhaps nowhere is this shift clearer than in welfare policy, which has long been structured by racist notions about who constitutes the "deserving" poor (Quadagno 1994). Recall that the New Deal policies created social security protections for large numbers of white Americans, but excluded farmworkers and domestic workers, who were largely people of color. Recall also that President Reagan widely tapped demonstrably untrue notions about black people abusing the welfare system, preferring "handouts" over employment. This is despite the fact that welfare assistance, even at that time, still did not support families beyond absolutely minimal subsistence, and was and is extremely difficult to gain and keep. Welfare reform in the 1990s, spearheaded by President Clinton, responded to these widespread sentiments, and also embodied this colorblind shift in its emphasis on personal responsibility and the widening of the use of welfare funds to include block grants (state funds for discretionary spending, little of which actually reaches poor families) and behavioral sanctioning (allowing caseworkers to enact penalties when they determine that a recipient is not compliant with a long list of challenging rules).

While caseworkers have always had the power to limit access to benefits for lack of compliance with behavioral rules, Monnat (2010) finds that race plays a significant role in the likelihood that women will receive sanctions that limit their access to benefits. Further, she emphasizes that "racialized labor market discrimination makes complying with TANF work requirements very difficult for these women" (701), given the prevalence of gender-specific racial stereotypes of black women. This is, she argues, reflective of colorblind applications of policy, where "caseworkers are unlikely to consider historical and structural disadvantage in their decisions to exempt participants from requirements or sanction them for noncompliance" (ibid.), especially when coupled with their own racial biases that shape their discretion in applying those sanctions. Similar dynamics shape the work of welfare rights advocates, where women of color are more willing to discuss and challenge the racial politics and controlling images of women on welfare in ways that white activists in the same movement often are not (Ernst 2010). In this way, colorblindness both drives and is perpetuated by the enforcement of welfare policy.

Disaster Response and International Politics

Colorblindness has also influenced disaster response. As other scholars of disaster (e.g. Eric Klinenberg) have noted, even natural disasters tend to reveal unnatural – that is, social – dynamics that deeply shape the way that disasters are felt and mitigated. Shelton and Coleman (2009) found that "those respondents who believed that whites and minorities had the 'same opportunities' and those who attributed 'black problems' to individual-level explanations were more likely to espouse antagonistic views toward the evacuees" (492) in Houston. Importantly, they also found that "many Houstonians (regardless of race/ethnicity) disguised their disdain for the Katrina evacuees behind widely held stratification beliefs such as 'equality' and 'individualism'" (493). Sweeney (2006) found nearly identical reactions to evacuees in Atlanta. Such notions are, of course, hallmark characteristics of colorblind ideology, and deeply shaped the ways that refugees are welcomed as potential threats or burdens more so than humans in need. The same notions seem to shape the reception of Syrian refugees in the United States and around the world in more recent years.

Indeed, on this global scale, fewer studies have traced colorblindness beyond the United States. However, Rhodes (2009) suggests that "While the UK and USA exhibit distinct processes of racial formation, the adherence to economic neoliberalism in both countries has resulted in the dominance of a political discourse that emphasizes the significance of ethnic and racial 'differences' rather than addressing systemic patterns of racist exclusion" (2.2). Specifically, he traces the existence of all four of Bonilla-Silva's (2003) frames in the UK's New Labour party's response to race riots in 2001. In France, the Census does not collect data on racial or ethnic identification, nor is it legal for any institutions, public or private, to collect this information. Léonard (2014) suggests that this absence, including in many social scientific studies, is not only upholding colorblind racism, but also implicitly and forcefully asserts "real" French identity as white identity.

Goldberg (2009) has termed these international responses to race relations as "racial americanization" [sic]. He writes:

> racial americanization is produced by seeming to do nothing special. This 'doing nothing special' consists of a mix of being guided by the presumptive laws of the market, the determinations of the majority's personal preferences, and the silencing of all racial preference with the exception especially of racial profiling for purported purposes of crime and terror control. The latter silencing fails to distinguish between exclusionary racist designs and practices, on one hand, and redressive or ameliorative racial interventions, on the other, reducing the latter to the former as the only contemporary racist expressions worth worrying about. (78–9)

It is a further entrenchment and institutionalization of colorblind ideology in all responses to racially infused dynamics. While more careful historical research suggests, as in the case of France, the makings of a colorblind national response to racial and ethnic changes were taking place at the same time as these shifts were beginning in the United States (Marker

2015), Goldberg's analysis still may be a useful way to understand the hegemony of US democratic notions and the free market on international race relations.

Discussion Question

- How could policy be universally applicable and still attentive to proven structural inequalities? What might this look like in education, housing, and other policies and programs?

Colorblindness in Culture

Colorblindness is not, however, limited to formal policy or institutional settings. Ideologies are implemented formally in policies and institutions, but they show up actively in our culture, in the everyday way that we talk and think about and interact with one another. As Rodriquez writes, "color-blind ideology is consequential for popular culture because it provides those with more racial power the discursive resources to decontextualize cultural objects from the histories and experiences from whence they came. At the same time, popular culture provides a venue in which color-blind ideology is itself produced and reproduced" (663–4).

Popular Culture

Interestingly, as Rodriquez's study also explores, this happens even in cultural spaces where race is put at the center, as can happen in music and comedy. For example, Pérez (2013) has shown the influence of colorblind ideology on comedian training, even when those comedians are seeking to challenge race-neutral norms. He writes, "Comedians frequently breach norms of etiquette and polite public discourse. With respect to race, stand-up comics often rely on blatant racial and ethnic stereotypes of the perceived deficiencies and proclivities of 'others.' Joke-tellers justify the use of such stereotypes by pointing out that the role of comedy is to confront touchy subjects, breach norms of etiquette, name taboos, etc." (479). Despite this, comedians learn to situate what are often still offensive racist remarks in ways that leave them public and unchallenged. Pérez argues that "such strategies are also intended to deny racism or racist intent in performances that engage in offensive racist discourse in public" (484).

Pérez's argument is also in part about how we perform racial identities and appropriate racial discourses. Rodriquez (2006) studied whites who are active in local, conscious hip-hop scenes. He argues that "by consuming hip-hop, members of the scene position themselves as 'cool' or hip by its association with African Americans, presenting themselves as confident, progressive whites smoothly moving through a cultural milieu of blackness" (646). Ironically, given the content of much of the music that they consume, he finds that they also do so in order to uphold colorblind frameworks, specifically by emphasizing how little race matters in their own lives.

Perhaps these earlier findings point toward the more recent recognition that scholars should better parse color-blind identity from colorblind ideology, for saying that race doesn't matter to one personally is different from saying that race does not matter politically. At the same time, in both of the above studies, this was also done to preserve or enhance a white racial self. For Rodriquez's (2006) participants, they attempted to "use hip-hop to position themselves in relation to their peers as savvy cultural insiders who are smoothly moving through a cultural milieu of blackness" (664). For Pérez's, they were able to baldly participate in overt racism by using other discursive maneuvers to distance themselves from its stigma. Either way, the focus remains on preserving the purity of a colorblind self rather than acknowledging or disrupting the realities of racism.

Home and Family Life

Of course, a perhaps more traditional way that color-blindness is deployed is in our everyday and "everynight"

(D. Smith 1990: 18) lives, particularly in our homes and family systems. Consider the case of domestic work. Moras (2010) finds that white women who hire domestic workers of a different race from their own often use colorblindness to justify the inequalities inherent in their relationships. She notes, following Bridget Anderson (2001), that there is a long history of the "dirty work" of household labor being divided along race and class lines. Despite this, "these relationships are often talked about in a seemingly non-racial manner, as white employers of domestic workers use cultural and linguistic markers to carve out alternative dimensions of racial privilege" (234), particularly by emphasizing immigration status and language. For example, the women she interviewed would rarely explicitly state racial preferences for their house cleaners, but would say that with European (e.g. Polish) women they felt a closer bond, and also found them to be "stronger" women than those from, for example, South America. At the same time, they also tended to stereotype Latina workers as better cleaners and harder workers.

Similar dynamics emerge in the context of transracial and transnational adoption. Notions about race deeply structure prospective parents' willingness to adopt across the color line, both generally and with regard to some specific races and/or nationalities (Treitler 2014). It also impacts upon the degree to which they are willing to confront the realities of their child, and themselves, as racialized subjects whose experiences and their resultant perspectives will differ based on the salience of race in modern societies. It is easy for white parents to believe that race truly does not matter, particularly when they have chosen to adopt across the color line. But these same parents may be unaware of the degree to which people of color still experience discrimination and exclusion, and given their life experience with racial privilege, may lack tools to help their child navigate this racist society.

Carla Goar (2014) studied some of the strategies that white adoptive parents have used when they do try to understand the significance of race in their children's lives, particularly those who participated in culture camps, which are designed to provide resources and support for adoptive families around areas of culture and tradition. But even there, she found a mix of colorblindness and racial awareness, not only among these families but often also inside of individual families. For example, families would equate race with other identities and experiences, or diminish its relevance altogether. Another scholar, Callahan, herself a transracial adoptee, asserts that "parents should not adopt across racial or cultural lines if they are unwilling or unable to help their child develop a whole and positive racial and cultural identity" (2014: 246). She suggests that prospective parents should examine the diversity of their communities, and take active measures to study and deeply consider the realities of inequalities, race, privilege, and the experience of both transracial adoptees, and people of color generally, before making such a choice. Otherwise, they can perpetuate the harm and isolation that she and many others experienced as a child of color inside of a white family and community.

Interracial Interactions

Colorblindness also has a way of traveling between formal and informal spaces, in our personal interactions with one another. However, those interactions tend to be deeply structured by the pervasive segregation, both residential and social, that shapes our lives – particularly the lives of whites, who experience higher levels of racial isolation than blacks and other people of color. Bonilla-Silva and Embrick (2007) argue that this creates a white habitus: "a racialized uninterrupted socialization process that conditions and creates whites' racial taste, perceptions, feelings, emotions, and views on racial matters" (324–5). They argue that this white habitus prevents whites from understanding their isolation and segregation as the result of racial dynamics, using instead a colorblind lens of preference or naturalization. This, of course, has consequences. They write, "Despite the Civil Rights revolution, whites, young and old, live fundamentally segregated lives that have attitudinal, emotional, and political implications" (341). Again, I found much the same thing among whites in stably racially diverse communities, who reproduced a white habitus inside of these diverse spaces that upheld the privileges of whites in communities that are ostensibly committed to racial diversity and progressive values (Burke 2012b).

Norton et al. (2006) found the same to be true in experimental interactions across the color line. Their participants indicated an unwillingness to acknowledge their ability to notice race, even when they were able successfully to use physical cues to sort people into racial categories – a process that is not alone racist! In particular, they "propose that the incongruity between trying to appear color-blind while automatically noticing color complicates strategic efforts to appear unbiased, creating an inevitable tension between efforts to achieve color blindness and actual success at doing so" (949). Their participants' logic seems to be that refusing to acknowledge the reality of socially constructed races forecloses the possibility that they can thus attach meanings to these racial markers, i.e. to be racist. They further write that "although we have focused on the negative impact for whites – on communication, performance, and self-presentation – these costs may ultimately extend to both whites and blacks, in the form of strained interracial interactions" (952).

All of the studies discussed in this section speak to the extent to which racial tensions, created primarily by whites' discomfort with the realities of racial categorizations and racial inequalities, create tremendous levels of denial and social distance, as well as the perpetuation of privileges, for whites. The chapters that follow will consider such "denials" more deeply, as they also reveal an awareness that many individuals actively choose to sidestep or ignore. But fundamentally they also both reflect and assert colorblind ideology. They reflect it in the often-genuine belief that race does not matter, and assert it in action and forms of race talk that are made on that basis. This protects the status

quo where whites can continue to glean unearned advantages, ranging from economic policy to personal comfort
and safety, and people of color are left grappling with unfair
systems and the stress and fatigue that comes from living in
a society that will not see their frustrations and challenges as
legitimate and worthy of support.

Discussion Questions

• Where and in what ways do you see colorblind ideologies
  employed in the informal social spaces that surround you?
• What are some of the harms of these often well-intentioned
  expressions?

Taking Stock of What We Know

This chapter has provided an overview of just some of the
many studies that have traced the presence and influence of
colorblind ideology and discourse in shaping the contemporary landscape of race relations, particularly in institutions,
policy and law, culture, and our interpersonal interactions.
It reveals the extent to which "the reproduction of social
hierarchies through mystification and obfuscation is perhaps
the most obvious and important function of the diversity
discourse" (Bell and Hartmann 2007: 905) – a diversity
discourse that, in the rare occasions that race is discussed,
often does so with deep ambivalence (Burke 2012a). That
is, while diversity discourse is often positive or, as Bell and
Hartmann (2007) have called it, "happy," it is coupled with
deep anxieties and ignorance on the part of many, especially
among whites.

It is in this way that, as Bonilla-Silva and Dietrich
(2011) have stressed, "coercion and violence are not the
central practices responsible for the reproduction of racial
domination in contemporary America" (174). Instead, it is a
denial of racism, an adherence to abstract ideals that ignore
the realities that prevent them, coded adherence to pervasive
racial stereotypes, social and residential isolation, and other

maneuvers that leave our current racial hierarchies and the assumptions that support them unchecked. This project, of documenting the presence and prevalence of this racial ideological system, has been a crucial one for us collectively as scholars, for "one aspect of the struggle against racial inequality must be to demystify this discourse, to look at how this seemingly benign discourse around race and the institutions that promote it, put their stamp on a continued racial project where whites benefit at the expense of the racialized Other" (Zamudio and Rios 2006: 484).

At the same time, as I have argued elsewhere (Burke 2016), there is a way in which this element of our collective work has become stagnant, given how convincingly we have already demonstrated the presence of this colorblindness in these many areas of our social and political life. The next phase of research, the new frontiers that are detailed in the following chapters, are now not only delving more deeply into the complexities and contradictions of colorblind racial ideology and discourse, including how the frames of color-blindness may be flexible or modified. They are also, perhaps more importantly, exploring the ways that a deeper consideration of the material conditions that produce, and are produced by, colorblind racism may reveal even more to us about the workings of contemporary racism. It is only when we take this next step that we will be able to move beyond identifying the presence of colorblind racism, and toward a deepened ability to challenge it.

Further Exploration

- Carefully study a school or workplace policy and consider how it can be improved for actual, rather than assumed, equity.
- Role play a challenge to an everyday interaction that is structured by colorblind ideology, so that you are better prepared to challenge it thoughtfully the next time you encounter something like it.

4

Contested Colorblindness

Despite the wide array of instances where colorblindness is deployed, it is far from monolithic. This chapter will explore the myriad ways that colorblindness is modified or abandoned by a range of social actors with varying social and political goals. That is, it demonstrates how colorblind ideologies and discourses are sometimes changed, in their expression or in their meaning, depending on the people using them or the social context where it is applied. This means that the expression of colorblindness is not always done uncritically, and is often shaped by additional contexts and strategies that reflect meaningful personal choices, and even resistance to the racial status quo. This recognition helps us to see how important it is to carefully explore social contexts and identities when studying racism, as this also helps us to understand the dynamics where racial inequality and violence take place. This chapter also, crucially, emphasizes that the emergence of this "new" racism has not meant an abandonment of the "old," that overt or other traditional forms of racism have themselves persisted or been modified. This complicates our understanding of how ideology and discourse interact with our social and political systems, and how differing outcomes and advantages are forged in a diverse racial landscape. It concludes by raising questions about the framework of colorblindness itself, setting the stage for the exploration of new frontiers in this area of study in the final chapter, which follows.

Variations Around and Across the Color Line

The first place to begin to unpack the complexities of color-blind ideologies and discourse, which help to constitute colorblind racism, is by exploring the variations both within and between racial groups. After all, colorblindness is not only pervasive among whites who may seek to defend their position in racial hierarchies. People of color also make use of colorblind ideologies, though typically less often and in ways that are different from those of whites. The context of interracial relationships – both romantic and platonic – also impact on the ways that colorblind frameworks are adopted by individuals or mobilized in specific social and political settings.

However, before beginning a discussion about the ways that the expression or enactment of colorblind racism differs for various racial groups, it is important to differentiate between the concepts of prejudice, racism, and ideology. While one could operationalize these terms in a variety of ways, generally most sociologists reserve the notion of "prejudice" or bias for individuals, and "racism" for patterned and institutional behaviors that support a system of racial inequality, and, in particular, white advantage. In this sense, while people of color can and often do hold biases to the same degree as whites, as the discussion below will make clear, it is difficult to support the argument that they act in ways that are racist. They have neither the social power nor can they often act in ways that confer unfair advantages to themselves as individuals or members of a race.

Ideology structures all of these dynamics, in that it provides a common-sense and ready-made worldview that "explains" some elements of social life in ways that are coherent to its adopters. Ideologies, like biases, stem from the process of socialization; we learn to understand the world around us in particular ways, and these understandings make increasing levels of sense to us the more often we hear them. This is no less true for people of color than it is for whites, given that, by and large, we all consume many of the same news sources, educational materials, and other forms of media. While one's lived experience as a person of color will necessarily shape one's view of the world, this is always in interaction with the larger societal messages that surround us. In short, we are all part of the same social system, and will therefore receive the same messages within it.

For example, Godfrey and Wolf (2016) conducted in-depth interviews with immigrant women and low-income women of color, and found that they tended to favor individual rather than structural explanations for their hardships, though often their responses included elements of both. That is, the women in their study were able to acknowledge structural issues such as racism and access to wealth and opportunities, but they also tended to blame themselves or others as individuals for the hardships that they endured. The researchers report, "fewer than half of respondents blamed structural factors for poverty and wealth, and these structural attributions were *always* paired with individual attributions" (101, emphasis added). So, even when structural or institutional factors were acknowledged, which would counter colorblind frameworks, individual factors were also emphasized, which affirms colorblind ideology.

A related finding from a national survey is that "A majority of both white and black respondents lean toward an individualist over a group-based orientation. Although the difference is statistically significant, it is very small in absolute terms (58.8 percent white v. 53.8 percent black) for the individualist view" (Manning, Hartmann, and Gerteis 2015: 538). That is, *most* white *and* black people support individually focused explanations for success, which is central to colorblindness. In particular, we can see how deeply the frame of abstract liberalism – which assumes equal opportunity and fairness and therefore emphasizes individual merit or drive, has permeated American culture.

The sections below will explore how various racial, and in some cases immigrant, groups navigate their perceptions of the racial landscape from within an ongoing system of disadvantage.

Black Americans

First, we will explore more deeply how this impacts upon the ways that black Americans navigate a racist society. While the above section emphasized abstract liberalism, one of the same studies found that cultural racism can be just as pervasive: "although blacks recognize structural discrimination to a much greater extent, they do not differ significantly from whites in terms of their embrace of cultural explanations for racial inequalities" (Manning, Hartmann, and Gerteis 2015: 541). The authors found that:

> More than 67 percent of whites rated the effect of 'effort and hard work' in explaining black disadvantage as important or very important, and 84 percent of whites said the same about the culture of black families. Yet the story is complicated by the fact that blacks were at least as likely to hold similar views about culture. Strikingly, there was *no statistically significant difference* between black and white responses on these last two items. (540, emphasis in original)

Bobo et al. seem to have anticipated this trend in 2012, when they wrote that "blacks are less and less likely to explain racial inequality in structural, discrimination-based terms" (75), instead tending to favor cultural or motivational explanations for racial inequality. Using survey data from the General Social Survey (GSS), they were also able to trace how support for affirmative action among black Americans has similarly declined. However, they suggest that more careful analysis with larger sampling among black Americans is necessary in order to parse out whether this is a result of cynicism, a collapse of group bonds, generally rising conservatism, or other possible factors.

Similarly, Welburn and Pittman (2012) conducted 45 in-depth interviews with middle-class African Americans and found that respondents draw upon both structural and motivational explanations for blacks' success. They find near-consensus that African Americans experience structural barriers to success, but that a majority also "believe that motivational factors including declining values, lack of effort and limited focus on educational attainment contribute to disadvantage for African Americans" (530). They offer these findings as support for what they call a "dual consciousness" – an ambivalence about racial matters (see Hunt 2007).

DeFreece (2014), in his study of black high-school seniors in a large metropolitan area, similarly found that "even among black youth who are prone to 'blame the system,' there is considerable variation in how they construct racial disadvantage, and therefore, in their developing stances toward racial justice" (46). He also emphasizes that "even among black youth who are the same age, attend the same school, live in similar neighborhoods, and hold similar basic ideological and identificational profiles, there is considerable divergence in constructions of racial disadvantage, bonds, and equality" (47). This important insight resists the notion that there are any homogenous views or uses of discourse among any one social group. Blacks are as diverse as any other group in their experiences and in their perceptions of reality; they may have no better evidence than any lay person about the realities of ongoing racism or the barriers that shape individual opportunities for success. This alone is not a problem – no one individual should carry the burden of representing or accounting for their group's aggregate attainment; the danger comes instead from the tendency to ask one representative of a group to do so, and to trust that perspective over decades and volumes of more careful social scientific research may demonstrate the opposite.

After all, much as Manning, Hartmann, and Gerteis found in their more recent (2015) study, Bonilla-Silva in 2003 found that many blacks see discrimination as central to their experiences in daily life, but then also attribute a lack of collective success to perceived cultural traits of other black Americans (158). That is, black Americans may have absorbed some of the biases that are socialized in a skewed media system and its narrow portrayals of black Americans, and/or may still attribute individual missteps to the influence of culture – as is common for many who disdain poverty, regardless of their racial identity. They do this even as they experience racism firsthand, with, as is common to us all, a perhaps greater appreciation for one's own circumstances than the assumed choices and circumstances of others. It is perhaps for this reason that, in *Racism Without Racists*, Bonilla-Silva's (2003) "main contention is that color-blind racism has affected blacks *indirectly* and that this has consequences for the likelihood of blacks developing an all-out oppositional ideology to color-blind racism" (152–3).

The complex ways that black Americans navigate a racist society and make sense of their own and others' successes and failures can also influence the degree to which one experiences the stress and trauma of racism. Coleman et al. (2012), counter to their own expectations, found that black college students who endorsed colorblind racial attitudes at higher rates also encountered less race-related stress. They suggest that this may be because a greater awareness of racism makes one likely to recognize it more often, cumulatively adding to the strain one experiences as a result. For example, Worthington et al. (2008) found that "irrespective of racial–ethnic minority status, perceptions of campus climate were found to be more positive when participants tended to deny the existence of racial privilege within intergroup relations" (16).

However, Coleman et al. also consider the possibility of intervening psychological strategies, and emphasize that "it is essential that one not assume that 'ignorance is bliss' and promote the socialization of colorblind racial attitudes as a good thing for African Americans" (499). Barr and Neville (2014), for example, found that "black young adults, who internalize color-blind racial beliefs, are negatively affected by Mainstream Socialization messages provided by parents.

In contrast, Black emerging adults, who acknowledge the reality of structural inequalities, are more able to successfully manage messages from parents concerning assimilating into mainstream culture" (160).

These choices also impact upon one's sense of self and the relationships with others in the same racial group: Neville et al. (2005) found that a greater acceptance of colorblind racial attitudes among blacks led to increased blame toward black Americans for social inequalities, acceptance of the status quo, and an internalization of anti-black stereotypes. She also found that those who identified more strongly with a critical race (structural) perspective tended to have stronger relationships with other African Americans. They write, "Racial ideology thus was reflected in friendship patterns, with those having less racial consciousness establishing closer interracial, compared to intra-racial, friendships" (41).

Latinxs

Those friendship patterns also impact upon the relationships between black Americans and other people of color. While racism negatively impacts upon the experiences of all people of color, pervasive anti-black sentiments are particularly salient, and can provoke non-black people of color to distance themselves from blackness as a strategy for survival and inclusion. For example, McClain et al. (2006) find that Latinxs stereotype black Americans at rates that rival or surpass those of whites. However, they may do so in order to distance themselves from racist associations with black Americans among whites, with whom they feel they have more similarities. Their longitudinal analysis also provides counterevidence for Bonilla-Silva's claim in his second edition (2006) of *Racism Without Racists* that the longer Latinxs are in the United States, the more they will identify with black Americans, though more research to test each claim is needed. Regardless, social distance from black Americans, they also remind us, is a strategy that non-black racial groups have regularly used in a variety of social contexts in order to navigate a racist society. Demonstrating that they are not like the assumed stereotypes of black Americans matters to other people of color.

For example, Korver-Glenn (2014) found that the cultural racism frame was widely used among Latinxs in a Texas community facing redevelopment, which she fears may have the unintended effect of supporting those redevelopment efforts. This may affirm the finding from Basler (2008) that Latinx naturalized citizens "often align themselves with 'whites' (and against blacks) in order to obtain the social and political capital inherent in whiteness" (125). She writes, "Perceptions of stigma associated with 'illegals' caused some naturalized citizens to distance themselves from a shared ethnicity with Mexican immigrants. They articulated this distance in racially disparaging language, emphasizing their 'whiteness', and vehemently opposing undocumented Mexican immigration" (158). In so doing, they demonstrate to whites that they are "one of the good ones" and therefore worthy of respect.

Dowling's book *Mexican Americans and the Question of Race* (2014) explored in depth how Mexican Americans view their own racial identities, and how they talk about race and racism. She finds that those Mexicans who identify as "white" on the US Census often wish to be seen as "Americans" rather than as racial subjects (e.g. Hispanic or Latinx), and believe that calling attention to race perpetuates racial divides. She asserts that "for 'white' Mexican Americans, part of vying for acceptance as an American means adopting the rhetoric of whiteness, including the use of color-blind ideology" (25). This group also tends to distance themselves from black Americans and immigrant Mexicans. Still, as she points out, "there are crucial differences ... between the uses and motivations behind how Mexican Americans employ color-blind ideology and the ways in which this framework is evoked by European Americans who claim not to see 'race'" (118).

For example, Mexican Americans also tend to discuss openly the realities of discrimination that they face, and to identify strongly with their cultural heritage. Skin color also does not seem to be a factor in determining the degree to which Mexican Americans identify with this "whiteness." In fact, she argues that it is racial discrimination rather than privilege that prompts identification with whiteness for these Mexican Americans. It is therefore a strategic and defensive use of colorblindness, not at all in fact "blind" to the realities of racism or used as a way to defend privileges – as it can be for so many whites. And, of course, this is just one end of a continuum she details in her book; many Mexican Americans take a consistently race-conscious and non-colorblind approach to their talking and thinking about race and their racial identities, though they, too, hesitate to talk about racism in some specific contexts.

Other People of Color/Immigrant Groups

All of this points to the reality that, for many people of color, particularly those who may be from immigrant communities, colorblind discourse is not adopted uncritically, as it may be for many whites who do not have to navigate a racist society that can cause one personal harm, or for whom a racial identity must be carved out from negative associations. Tatum and Brown (2016) write that, for example, "rather than 'assimilating' through colour-blind or colour-conscious ideologies, first-generation Dominican immigrants may develop a colour-blind approach in reaction against the American racial system" (8). This racial system is one that carries aggregate benefits for whites and disadvantages for people of color, no matter one's individual racial ideology or identity.

It is perhaps for this reason that O'Brien (2008) refers to the ways that Latinxs and Asians reproduce the framework of colorblindness as "color-nuanced ... to highlight the ways in which the racial middle draws on nuances of ethnic differences within racial categories more regularly than other research has found with whites or blacks" (63). For example, Asians and Latinxs adopt naturalization frames at rates nearly equal to whites, but abstract liberalism at rates closer to that of blacks. O'Brien emphasizes, however, that this is not a mix of "white" and "black" strategies for talking about race, but rather a distinct form of racial expression. Further, "many may tiptoe around generalized assumptions about African Americans but feel more comfortable relying on stereotypes both for other ethnic groups within their own racial category and for other categories in the racial middle of which they are not members" (94). And half of her sample of those populations did not reproduce colorblindness at all.

It is in this way that Campón and Carter (2015) suggest that "shifting the reference from internalized racism to appropriated racial oppression captures the multidimensional and complex nature of the process of the internalization of negative racial stereotypes in people of color, as well as the sociocultural, psychological, and historical components of that process" (498). The scale that they developed to measure appropriated racial oppression includes a measure for "patterns of thinking that maintain the status quo" (ibid.), which is another way of conceptualizing colorblindness. But this is merely one measure, which, as their comment above emphasizes, cannot capture the myriad ways that people of color may internalize, appropriate, make nuanced, or otherwise modify the larger ideology of colorblindness.

For example, Chen et al. (2006) found much variation among Asian Americans in the degree to which they identified racially, experienced racism, and subscribed to colorblind or other racial ideologies. Those experiences are far from homogenous, nor are they a simple internalization of the status quo. Even so, Pendakur (2015) considers the extent to which Asian Americans may be primed toward colorblindness, given their positioning relative to the Model Minority stereotype. That is, many Asians may embrace a "positive"-seeming stereotype that imagines a culture of hard work and intelligence, particularly in a racist society that uses this Model Minority stereotype both to support cultural racism generally and to punish black Americans, whose culture is imagined to be deficient, specifically. While his interview sample was small, he found that most of his Asian American participants had internalized the model minority stereotype, particularly their status as "honorary whites." He also found that they largely adhered to the logic of colorblind racism. Similarly, Korgen (2009) finds that middle- and upper-class biracial Americans with a white and black parent embrace an "honorary white" racial identity, distancing themselves from pervasive stereotypes, which they largely affirm, of poor blacks. While this reflects a troubling degree of individual bias and internalized racism, it can also be read as a strategy to position oneself via one's imagined culture in order to lessen the impact of racism on one's own life.

Similarly, another study of Korean American entrepreneurs showed that this population used three of the four frames of colorblind racism – minimization, cultural racism, and abstract liberalism (Nopper 2010). For this group, an effort to embrace a multicultural immigration narrative – one that emphasizes and attempts to celebrate cultural differences, perhaps unintentionally also denies structural and institutional inequalities of opportunity in the immigration and economic systems. For example, since 1965 select Koreans, and many other Asian Americans, have received preferences in a newly configured immigration system that favors individuals who have the education and personal means to contribute to "desirable" areas of the economy such as business, science and technology, and more. This is a result of the social and economic factors in the sending society, and not simply of a "culture" of hard work or any natural talents in these fields. Further, prior to 1965, the immigration system largely barred Asians, and many were working class or poor – thus leaving a large pool ready and eager to immigrate to the USA for the first time in larger numbers, creating a sudden increase in this population working in these fields. As I often tell my students, the "culture" of Asians (itself not monolithic) didn't suddenly change after 1965; rather, the structure of the immigration system changed to allow opportunities for select individuals and families that had been closed to them previously.

White Americans

The role of culture and ethnic or national affiliation is less often studied among whites, likely given the diminished salience of ethnicity in shaping whites' daily lives and opportunities when compared to pre-World War II eras, when many white ethnics were seen as distinct communities and even as not fully white (see Brodkin 1998). Even so, recent research by Monica McDermott (2015) suggests that those white Americans who still identify with a European national or cultural group (i.e. "ethnicity") will make sense of race differently from whites who do not, though both still tend to uphold colorblind frames. "Color-blind identities may be contingent," she writes, "giving way according to context or cue to an overtly color-visible identity. These color-visible identities are then used to counter non-White claims for redress or equal rights" (1468). Even so, "Color visibility is not necessarily linked to a progressive racial ideology that is the converse of color-blind racism" (1467).

She also pays attention to the increasing trend among whites to actually claim a racial identity, itself a move that breaks in some ways from a colorblind impetus to see oneself as an individual or perhaps as an "American" – for which whiteness is often uncritically assumed. She emphasizes that education does not seem to have an effect on these kinds of responses, meaning that "the response of 'White' to the ancestry question does not represent a failure to understand the intent of the question but rather a conscious affiliation with a racial rather than a national origin identity. White identity may be becoming the new norm for populations across rural America, perhaps replacing American identity in some quarters" (1469).

Perhaps similarly, in a study of "contested whites" – those who consider themselves white but are not always considered to be white by others, Vargas found that "colour-blindness is also prevalent and arguably even stronger at the margins of whiteness. So, while the Irish disassociated themselves from blacks nearly a century ago in an effort to achieve whiteness ... those at the margins today appear to disassociate themselves from the concept of race altogether – writing it off as a topic unworthy of concern or discussion" (2014: 22–95). Certainly this is fodder for much ongoing research, possibly longitudinal and comparative as this liminality may change for this group; they may come to experience the US racial system in ways similar to immigrant or other populations. Even so, it suggests that even where colorblindness is pervasive – in the sense that race is irrelevant – it also takes distinct forms. After all, this kind of expression is not necessarily or exclusively one of racism.

It is also important, on this note, to point out that, as Manning, Hartmann, Gerteis (2015) find, "only 23.1% of whites agreed that 'Race no longer matters in the USA'" (539). In fact, "a significant number of white Americans do *not* completely minimize the existence of racism" (543, emphasis added). "More than half of whites and about two-thirds of blacks disagree or strongly disagree that equal opportunity exists for everyone" (538). This is an important finding, and a related study by some of the same authors, which will be explored in depth in the next chapter, flies in the face of the notion, popular among many academics and at times explicitly stated by Bonilla-Silva, that most whites adhere to and uncritically adopt colorblind ideologies. Many, these authors find, do not.

Of course, the logic of colorblindness still holds tremendous institutional and cultural power, as the last chapter explored in depth. And, certainly, colorblindness is a common defense utilized by many to support the racist status quo. The inequality that reflects that logic is deeply entrenched, and continues to grow. Still, it is crucial that we begin to acknowledge that colorblindness is not homogenous among whites any more so than it is for other racial and social groups. The fact that so many whites understand and acknowledge the reality of unequal opportunities by race in this country is a significant one to grapple with, especially given that the needle has not moved on inequality as a result. Perhaps this is because, as Leonardo and Zembylas (2013) point out,

> One of the technologies of whiteness is its ability to project itself as its own alibi. In other words, Whites have built anti-racist understandings that construct the racist as always someone else, the problem residing elsewhere in other Whites. In some instances, this alibi is a white subject's former self. In a recuperative logic, whiteness is able to bifurcate whites into "good" and "bad" subjects, sometimes within the same body or person during public race dialogue. (151)

My own research (Burke 2012a) has explored how whites in diverse urban communities often situate themselves as "one of the good ones" (see also Burke 2017) while still individually and collectively taking action to protect their personal privileges and comforts, reproducing a white habitus inside of these racially diverse communities (Burke 2012b). These findings all suggest the need to grapple deeply not just with whiteness but also with the complex role of racial identities as they relate to ideology and discourse – explored in some depth as a frontier for new research possibilities in the next chapter.

Discussion Questions

- How does one's racial identity and life circumstances impact upon the way colorblind discourse can be heard and understood?
- What insights about our social and racial systems emerge from this more complex reading of colorblind expressions among these diverse groups?

Variations in Social Contexts

Racial identity is not the only factor that creates variations and contingencies in the belief in or expression of colorblind discourses and ideologies. Other social categories such as class, age, family and relationship structures, religion, politics, and more all help to paint a more complex picture about the nature and expression of colorblind ideologies, as we are exploring in this chapter. And, as the next chapter will explore in greater depth, this points to the ways that ideology is rarely fixed, but rather contingent on the social context in which it is both learned and expressed. Examining these terrains will help us to better understand the dynamics of contemporary racism, and thus provide us with the foundations needed to better challenge it.

Interracial Intimacy

For example, Jessica Vasquez (2014) finds that whites in interracial marriages are often prompted by these shared experiences to appreciate the salience of race in ways that they previously, or otherwise, might not. However, even there, the context of these experiences shapes the expression of and adherence to colorblind frameworks: "public situations of discrimination or inequality stimulate race cognizance whereas private sphere themes encourage colorblindness. Second, duration of marriage also influences racial consciousness, the more recently married typified by colorblindness and the long-lasting marriages characterized by race cognizance" (279).

Perhaps similarly, Goar, Davis, and Manago (2017) explore the degree to which white parents who adopt children of color express colorblind or race-conscious world-views and parenting strategies. They find that most often parents in these families do both, showing how "people draw deftly upon available cultural frames in ways that both resist and reinforce racist hierarchies" (348). And yet, part of this adherence to colorblindness in relationships or family systems may also stem from the societal resistance that those in interracial relationships still face. Erica Chito Childs (2006), in her comprehensive study of black–white interracial relationships, found that most whites adhere to colorblind frameworks in their resistance to interracial relationships, perhaps believing that intra-racial preferences are natural (rather than socially imposed) or by adhering to frames of cultural racism. Blacks' resistance, on the other hand, more often comes from a place of racial identity and pride; they may be affirming the value of one's blackness in a society that otherwise diminishes it. Here, even resistance to interracial relationships, which can sound like adherence to a racist status quo, is shaped by one's racial identity and racial experiences.

Friendship patterns may also have an impact on the degree to which colorblind ideology is manifested. Vanessa Gonlin and Mary E. Campbell (2017) explore the degree to which people of color's use of colorblind ideology is impacted by close relationships with whites, which they acknowledge could travel in either causal direction. That is, close relationships with whites could cause people of color to absorb the colorblind racial attitudes that many whites hold, or, holding these colorblind racial attitudes may prompt some people of color to forge closer relationships with whites than with people of color. They find that "although there is not a consistent pattern of greater levels of CBRI attitudes for all groups across all measures, people of color with close relationships with whites are more likely to endorse specific attitudes that minimize the amount of racism faced by racial minorities, even controlling for other characteristics of the respondents" (938). In particular, people of color who have close relationships with whites tend to minimize what *other* groups experience as racism.

Even when an interracial friendship does help to develop a greater awareness of racist realities, it may not spur antiracist social action. Korgen and O'Brien (2006) write that, among forty black–white friendship pairs, "although all the white friends attained more positive outlooks toward blacks, few became antiracist activists through their close friendship with a black person" (283). They also tended to focus on their similarities, much like many of the interracial couples and families discussed above, and to ignore race-based differences. "Doing so enabled them to avoid the discomfort of having to acknowledge their differences and allowed them to experience the interpersonal attraction common among the majority of same-race close friends" (ibid.). In this way, colorblindness is being replicated, but segregation is not – complicating the notion that colorblindness always leads to racist outcomes.

Intergenerational transfer also does not happen in ways that thinking about colorblindness only as a socialization process supporting racism might imply. Hagermann (2016) suggests that "children interpret frames of colorblind ideology and then make these frames their own, sometimes reproducing these frames as presented, sometimes reworking them into something new, and sometimes even rejecting these frames altogether" (68). While children hold dramatically less influence over social outcomes, it is still important to notice the agency that all of us, children included, assert in both shaping and being shaped by the ideological frameworks that surround us.

Intersectionality and Politics

This also complicates the notion that whites are always acting out of malice or ignorance when discussing race or even using colorblind frames. While colorblind racism is deployed in the service of whiteness generally, whiteness is always interacting with other social and political identities that can complicate the ways that it is adopted or expressed among whites. Research has shown that one's social-class position shapes the frames that resonate with whites, and those that they may choose to strategically employ. Ramsaran (2009) finds that "middle-class whites are more likely to shroud their arguments about issues of race using ... the minimization lens and the cultural lens to justify their positions," (290) but rarely naturalization or abstract liberalism. Abstract liberalism and naturalization, however, were the primary frames used by working-class whites in his study. Bonilla-Silva (2003), after all, had suggested that working-class women might be the least likely among whites to embrace colorblindness (2003), though empirical evidence supporting on this claim, such as that of Ramsaran's above, is mixed.

Here we already see class and gender interacting to shape the expression of colorblind racism. Political framing adds an additional layer. The history of colorblindness as expressed in things like the Southern Strategy, as well as the contemporary emergence of the alt right, might imply that colorblindness is inherently connected to conservatism. But liberals can be just as colorblind as conservatives. My own research has shown that even in communities who pride themselves on diversity and progressive politics, colorblind framing is widespread, and shapes social action in ways that continue to privilege whites (Burke 2012a). Similarly, Hughey (2012) has shown that racist discourse, including colorblindness, exists even among whites who attempt to be explicitly antiracist. And as Angie Beeman (2015) writes, "it is more than just white nationalists who co-opt colorblind language or liberal antiracists who engage in paternalistic colorblind ideology that contribute to the problem. Radical leftist European Americans and people of color who do not engage in the usual tropes of color-blind ideology and are conscious of how racism works can also participate in the same racism evasiveness, which maintains the racial status quo" (144).

Further considering the political left, Bonilla-Silva and Dietrich (2011) have traced President Obama's complicity with colorblind frames and racist outcomes, and like many others, take a critical stance toward those who imagine that President Obama was a harbinger of racial progress, ushering in a supposed "post-racial" era. At the same time, they acknowledge that "for older generations of blacks desperate to see racial equality before they die, and for many post-Reagan generation blacks and minorities who have seen very little racial progress in their lifetimes, Obama became the new messiah of the Civil Rights movement" (198).

This is also connected to the dynamics in black churches, which played an important historical role in racial justice movements. However, survey research shows a marked decline in black churches' participation in social protest movements in recent years (see Barber 2011). While there is certainly no monolithic response to racial dynamics in the black community or among black churches, Barber (2011) found that the class standing of the church members seems to influence the degree to which these churches frame relevant social issues as structural rather than individual – that is, along race-cognizant or colorblind frames. Similarly, Cobb et al. (2015) find that "Blacks [who] attend religious services in multiracial congregations are significantly less likely than either Whites in multiracial congregations ... or Blacks in more racially homogenous congregations to endorse structuralist understandings of racial inequality" (195). They also find that "Blacks in multiracial congregations are less structuralist, relative to their white counterparts ..., while Hispanics in multiracial congregations are more structuralist" (ibid.).

Surely there are, and will continue to be more, studies that present shades and variations to the expression of colorblindness as new strains of research move forward, and as the racial landscape continues to change. Even so, the contexts above already illustrate that the application of colorblind frames and ideology are not always direct or uncritical, and instead are often shaped by additional variables and strategies that reflect agency and even resistance to the racial status quo. The flip side of this, of course, is that the same level of agency can be applied toward efforts to bury racism just below the surface of acceptable discourse, or to obscure it from public view or attachment to specific individuals. Those strategies take place in the use of coded racism and racism in anonymous or private spaces.

Discussion Questions

- What factors seem to spur social action around colorblind ideals versus colorblind ideologies?
- How have you seen colorblind ideologies reflected in ways that are more complicated than a simple uncritical defense of racism?

Backstage Racism, Racial Codes, and Overt Expressions

Given the above, it is important also to emphasize that, as Picca and Feagin (2007) write, "The old racist stereotypes have *not* disappeared. Many whites still accept at least a few of these racist stereotypes publicly in replies to pollsters and researchers. Antiblack images, cognitive stereotypes, and emotions remain important in most whites' consciousnesses" (*x*). This reality also causes some, as do Picca and Feagin in their book *Two-Faced Racism: Whites in the Backstage and Frontstage* (2007), to assert that the framework of a "new" racism is flawed. After all, as Chapter 2 explored, "color-blind" frames around abstract notions like equality and justice have long been used in racially exclusionary ways. What is even more concerning, strong, overt racism, particularly anti-blackness, has remained pervasive and seems to be gaining a resurgence in recent years in a number of Nazi-influenced and other white supremacist movements both in the USA and around the world. As such, it is worth exploring the contours of some of these expressions.

Backstage Racism

Even when it is not overt, it is clear that racism has not become fully colorblind, but rather that "much of the overt expression of blatantly racist thought, emotions, interpretations, and inclinations *has gone backstage* – that is, into private settings where whites find themselves among other whites, especially friends and relatives" (Picca and Feagin 2007: *x* – emphasis in original). They find many

> whites in backstage settings acting as though their racist performances are normal, expected, and commonplace. This is true not only for private interactions among white friends and family members but also usually with white strangers. For these whites, the backstage is safe from many contemporary frontstage expectations in regard to racial matters

and thus often a preparation for frontstage interactions for people of color. (241)

In this sense, there is nothing colorblind in these expressions of racism.

That said, the negotiation of the front and back stage still upholds this new racial order. As Kristin Myers (2005) writes,

> Beneath the superficial colorblindness … lies a more careful racism that is markedly similar to the previous racism of the old … People selectively choose their audience, transferring old ideas in new ways. People creatively locate and/or construct pockets of respite from what they might conceptualize as 'thought police,' censors who seek to quash racetalk altogether. In these refuges, old racist ideas are renewed and accepted as largely legitimate, thereby insulating the [ideas] from challenge. (207)

Anyone who has overheard an offensive joke, a burst of racist frustration, or a bold proclamation of taboo racist speech can attest to both the ongoing reality of "old-school" racism and the impact of its transgression when it is expressed.

It is for this reason that many are so defensive when such expressions are uttered, for example by celebrities or politicians who are caught and sanctioned for racist language. These slips or gaffes are defended as just that, a deviation from the otherwise pure language of someone who, they insist, is therefore falsely labeled as a racist. But as Jane Hill (2008) writes, "Once the label is applied, the intricate personalist discourse of motives … takes over as a form of common sense, and makes serious critical discussion of white racism extremely difficult. Since racism is located 'in the heart,' it is difficult to detect" (116). She emphasizes that this way of defending one's racist transgressions also keeps the focus on racism in the individual rather than in the institutional realm. Sarah Mayorga-Gallo (2016) has made a similar point, writing, "Claims of color blindness are popularly understood as markers of racial tolerance in this new post-Civil Rights era, particularly because racism is commonly perceived to be an individual trait. In the 'postracial' era, common sense dictates that racists are bad and ignorant people and that color blindness helps individuals to avoid the 'racist' label" (n.p.). Racism becomes about bad people, or more often, good people occasionally saying bad things, rather than pervasive ideologies of white supremacy and the institutions that support it.

Coded Racism

This careful defense of racist speech and acts is not only retroactive. Alongside colorblind racism we have also seen a rise in the use of racial codes – an extension, as Omi and Winant (2015) write, of colorblind ideologies: "The rise of 'code word' strategies was a logical next step, an effort to race-bait less explicitly, while making full use of the traditional stereotypes. 'Code words' like 'get tough on crime' and 'welfare handouts' reasserted racist tropes of black violence and laziness without having to refer to race at all" (218). Coded talk may on the surface appear to be difficult to analyze – but its success depends on its pervasive familiarity and implicitly shared meanings, a method I use to analyze racial codes in my research: usually it is traceable when the effort is made to do so. Even so, Jane Hill (2008) argues that "deep principles determine what components of the message are explicit, and what components are recovered through inference" (33).

These inferences must resonate with their intended audience if they are to be successful as codes, and are often tapped by those who want to further specific political goals: "Strategic racism refers to purposeful efforts to use racial animus as leverage to gain material wealth, political power, or heightened social standing" (López 2014: 46). López suggests that such expressions are not primarily about racism, but rather the pursuit of another political or economic goal. Even so, coded racism becomes central to those projects, as my own work on the Tea Party's use of racist tropes around welfare, national security, and immigration make clear (Burke 2015). After all, as Myers (2005) notes, "Formal changes have made the public expression of certain ideas politically incorrect, but their expression endures in the private realm: an unofficial classroom where the old ways can be nurtured, innovated, and passed on with little scrutiny or castigation" (3).

Racist Jokes

The ongoing practice of racist joking is another avenue where the framework of colorblindness is simultaneously perpetuated (in the assertion that one is "just kidding") and altered (by furthering either overt racism or racist assumptions in the joke itself). While, as Cabrera (2014b) notes, "One racial joke does not deny a person of color admissions to a university or subject a person to racial violence ... the problem lies in the underlying ideologies and attitudes that make the joke funny" (10). Cabrera also notes, in his study of white male college students' racial humor, that whites' relative social distance from people of color makes it so that whites remain protected from sanctions or criticisms of this kind of racist joking. This happens even on college campuses, which are typically celebrated for their diversity when compared to the segregation in the communities that surround them. He suggests that

> hegemonic Whiteness creates the condition that normalizes the experiences and views of White people. This, in turn, allows for racial joke telling and White racial enclaves to be framed as innocuous and nonracist. These behaviors (joke telling) and environments (White space) are contextualized within an ideological orientation that blames minorities for injecting race into nonracial situations (minority sensitivity). (12)

These practices create space for explicitly racist speech (via jokes) to comfortably take place within the rules of a color-blind ideological and social system.

In a similar vein, Raúl Pérez (2013) studied standup training for comics, and found that they tend to "make racist discourse palatable by learning to employ certain strategies of talk which are intended to circumvent the current 'constraints' on racial discourse in public" (479). As this form of racist expression takes hold, he urges us to remember that

> The point, however, is not only that peripheral 'genuine' racists might be emboldened through the mainstreaming of racist comedy, but the unique and frequently unchallenged (re)production of racism *through* humor more generally fits within the larger logic of a shifting racial discourse in public. (499)

A more recent study of Pérez's (2017) explores how humor is one way that people in fact display race consciousness, often as a deliberate affront to colorblind principles and ideologies or even "political correctness," given that people often defend racist humor by using colorblind principles such as being "equal-opportunity offenders." But as Embrick and Henricks (2013) also emphasize, jokes, slurs, and racial epithets are both pervasive and racially unequal. Pérez (2017) points to racist humor in police departments, which seems pervasive, as a prime example of this kind of power disparity. This creates the absurd idea that it's political correctness, and not racial violence, that is somehow the real concern.

Overt Racism

And that violence, of course, seems only further emboldened in the wake of mass protest to police violence, in the rise of Trump and the alt-right, and given the movement of racism into online spaces, especially given how widely people interact and engage online. For example, as of Fall 2017, the Southern Poverty Law Center had tracked 917 active hate groups in the United States (SPLC 2017). Given that in 2016 Pew Research Center found that a majority of adults get at least some of their news online (Pew 2016), this creates a troubling landscape where racial hatred and misinformation can become pervasive. King and Leonard 2014 write, "Struggles for racial justice made overt racism, segregation, and stratification problematic, if not impossible. In their wake, white power was reworked, fostering visible and virulent forms pushed to the margins as well as nearly invisible and more insidious variants at the center of everyday life" (20).

Much of this overtly racist organizing takes place online. As King and Leonard (2014) write, "In a very real sense, the World Wide Web has nurtured the growth of a white supremacist-nationalist popular (sub)culture. Specifically, online sites have enabled individuals and institutions spaces through which to create and consume white power" (8). One of the prominent scholars of both internet studies and racism, Jessie Daniels, notes that "race and racism persist online in ways that are both new and unique to the Internet, alongside vestiges of centuries-old forms that reverberate both offline and on" (2013: 696). Daniels also notes in some of her other work (2009a) that the existence of some immensely popular white supremacist websites reflects an ongoing and pervasive need for many whites to affirm their racial superiority and connect in an intentional community that shares those values.

This is particularly important given the pressures of colorblind ideologies, where overt racism is not only thought to be a relic of the past, but also carries social sanctions. As such, as Kettrey and Laster (2014) note, "online displays of overt racism can be explained by the fact that the Web offers users a sense of privacy and anonymity that, whether actual or simply perceived, allows them to express themselves in ways that they would not normally do so publicly" (258). They go on to explain how colorblind and overt racism may hold one another up: "users utilized overt rhetoric to lay claim to white spaces, while color-blind rhetoric distorted efforts among users to deconstruct racism" (269). In this way, even overt racism can reflect societal pressures toward colorblindness.

Online media such as gaming have also replicated the many racial (and gendered) stereotypes that are prevalent in society, such as representing African Americans as "gangbangers." Created and developed predominantly by white men, these images are reflective of the worldviews and racial stereotypes that they have absorbed and therefore reproduce. As Daniels and LaLone (2012) write:

> These ... games are a primarily white interpretation of African American culture for white people to play. In this way, video games represent a way in which systemic racism is expressed differently than in the offline world. The creation of a private sphere to explore the thoughts and values game makers put into their games allows players to explore certain aspects of their racially motivated beliefs that they may not know or understand they have. (93)

As such, this seemingly innocuous space of "play" and gaming carries a very real risk of reproducing racist tropes and cementing associated racial stereotypes. The same is often true of sport (see Hawkins 2015). For example, an examination of online message boards devoted to English football reveals "a deep, essentialist view of national belonging and identity that is primarily centered on whiteness and the rejection of multiculturalism" (Cleland 2013: 3).

Even when the intent is not to produce overt racist expressions or a community for hate and white supremacy online, the presence of these communities and expressions creates the potential for recruitment through propaganda into that space. Cloaked websites, in particular, deliberately conceal the politics of the author or organization who administers the site as a form of propaganda. These sites therefore serve as covert racist propaganda. After all, "it is not only possible but likely that casual or novice web users could come across racist propaganda inadvertently while looking for legitimate... information" (Daniels 2009b: 672). As Daniels suggests, this is particularly troubling when we consider younger readers' ability to discern truths about racism and forge paths toward justice on that basis. Certainly this has become relevant in the era of "fake news" and what some are now calling, in the Trump era of "alternate facts," "post-truth" politics. In this way, old and new media blend features of old and new racism. And as Daniels (2009a) suggests, "More sinister than possible recruitment is the Internet's capacity to globally link white supremacists, regardless of national boundaries, thus affirming translocal white identity" (7).

Discussion Questions

- What do ongoing overt expressions of racism reveal about current racial dynamics?
- How do these expressions relate to movements for social and racial justice?

New Questions about the New Racism

It is becoming increasingly clear that while colorblindness constitutes a "new" form of racism, it is neither fully applied nor is it a fixed ideology that is practiced in ways that do not vary by speaker, context, or location. It is for this reason that scholars are now beginning to turn our attention to the ways that racial ideologies morph alongside shifting social contexts and in response to very real challenges. Given the rise of the far right and a resurgence of white supremacist movements in the United States and many other countries in recent years, it is all the more urgent that we pay careful attention to the multiple and shifting dynamics of racism. One of those dynamics is the persisting ideology of colorblindness – both as an aspiration as well as a set of false assumptions about the nature of racial inequality. But colorblindness sits alongside other racial ideologies, and other social and political pressures that are forever responding to and also impacting changing social dynamics. The final chapter, which follows, will explore these new frontiers in the study of colorblind and contemporary racism and how those insights can spur movement for social change.

Further Exploration

- List two or three questions that emerge for you in the consideration of colorblind racism in this chapter, and consider how they might be empirically studied.
- Research information literacy skills to improve your ability to discern fake news and media bias. One great place to start is webliteracy.pressbooks.com.

5

New Directions

The last chapter explored a range of nuances and competing realities that complicate any straightforward application of colorblind ideology and discourse to our everyday social life. Some of this reflects elements in our culture that may indeed be changing. For example, Bobo et al. (2012) analyze GSS data and suggest that there has been "a sweeping fundamental change in norms regarding race. A Jim Crow-era commitment to segregation, explicit white privilege, revulsion against mixed marriages, and the categorical belief that blacks were inherently and biologically inferior to whites [may have] collapsed" (74). At the same time, as recent events have shown, there may be a resurgence of traditional forms of racism and an insistence on white supremacy. Michael Tesler's (2012) research, for example, demonstrates how "old-fashioned racism" played a role in many white Americans' voting preferences during the Obama era. Since then, the alt right in the United States evokes a range of both colorblind and race-conscious strategies, but their connections to overtly white supremacist groups seems clear. Given all of this, many Americans are grappling with how to make sense of a politicized racial climate in the United States.

After all, colorblindness is explicit when we say that "all lives matter" in response to the Black Lives Matter movement, which arose in order to call attention to deep and well-demonstrated racial disparities in policing and the criminal justice system. At the same time, many white Americans, thanks to the work of organizers in the Black Lives Matter movement, are now willing to see and talk about the realities of racism, demonstrating more awareness of racism than they had in recent decades. This prompts confusion for those who are trying to talk about race, given the *ideal* of colorblindness – that race should not matter – alongside growing recognition that it does. Similarly, in neighborhoods, schools, businesses, and more, many *desire* diversity, but still replicate racist practices and, knowingly or not, reproduce advantages for whites. How do we grapple with these contradictions and competing realities?

All of these phenomena have led many sociologists to begin to explore new lines of research around colorblind racism. As this book, particularly Chapter 3, has made clear, there is a well-established body of scholarship that has utilized this framework in order to explore the ways that colorblind ideologies and discourses have impacted our culture, institutions, and interpersonal relationships. However, as I have argued previously, "much of the literature has become stagnant, repeatedly identifying the presence of its frames without adding new insights" (Burke 2016: 103). New approaches to studying colorblind and contemporary racism can help us to better understand concretely how colorblind racism might impact upon social outcomes (Hughey et al. 2015), how it can change and adapt to new realities (Doane 2014), its real-world roots and consequences (Bonilla-Silva 2015; Burke 2016), and more. These all speak to the need to ensure that when we study colorblind racism, we do so in ways that are attached to what is always a changing social environment. After all, as Omi and Winant (2009) write, "the very necessity of divulgating a 'color-blind' racial ideology itself demonstrates that deep fissures have appeared in the 'system' of racism, and that it is not as monolithic as [previous] authors have suggested" (2009: 123).

There are a number of new trajectories emerging for research into colorblind and contemporary racism. This chapter will explore new ways of conceptualizing color-blindness, how typical practices of whiteness continue to subvert progress, and what resistance to racism might look like, given these trends.

Colorblind Variations, Identities, and Continuums

New research is beginning to make helpful distinctions between the many ways that colorblindness has been concep-tualized. Typically, for example in Bonilla-Silva's (2003) framework, colorblindness is about denying the realities of racism and defending white privilege by blaming people of color for structural inequalities or assuming that things like segregation are the result of natural, and therefore neutral, human impulses. But as a growing body of recent scholarship suggests, not all people think about or use the discursive frames of colorblindness this way. For example, Jessica Vasquez's research demonstrates that "intermarried couples invoke colorblindness *optimistically,* signaling a moment when race/ethnicity does not inhibit relations or bespeak inequality" (2014: 276). She goes on to suggest that "colorblindness literature oversimplifies racial consciousness by conceiving of it as dichotomous: one either is race conscious or colorblind. This bivariate conceptualization of mental constructs around race is unrealistically sharp and nullifies the possibility that people may view race as a powerful principle of social organization in certain circum-stances but not others" (276).

This insight is important in many ways, perhaps most centrally because it makes room for subjectivities – how people make sense of their own lives and worlds – in analyses of racism. It is in some sense understandable that our study of contemporary, and especially colorblind, racism had turned away from subjectivities. As Chapter 2 demonstrated, for much of the history of the study of race in sociology, the study of racism was only rooted in the study of individual attitudes and beliefs. It was therefore important in recent decades to insist that structural, institutional, and ideological mechanisms were deeply shaping the hearts and minds of individuals, in ways that, particularly for whites, obscured the realities of racism and protected privileges. Even so, as Vasquez (2014) writes, "The field of Whiteness studies has conceived of Whiteness as an overly uniform racial identity. [Her] study has shown that rather than being immutably invested in White privilege and nonracial outlooks, the racial consciousness of intermarried Whites is remarkably varied" (288). In a similar vein, she also writes that "Colorblindness literature is unrealistically bivariate, obscuring middle ground between racial progressivism and colorblind racism ... Further, colorblindness has previously only been theorized as neoconservative and racist" (288). Her study examining the racial ideologies of whites who are married to people of color suggests a much more complex, contingent, and varied middle ground than these prior frameworks would suggest.

This careful attention to individual subjectivities is helping us to better understand how people actually make sense of race and racism in their private lives and in the public sphere, which can help us to analyze those dynamics and how they might be changing. One of these contributions is in recent research by Hartmann et al. (2017), who parse out color-blind ideals from colorblind ideology. This distinction helps researchers to move away from the assumption that color-blind discourse always reflects a defense of racism. While certainly that has *often* been true, their work recognizes how people may also explicitly and actively choose colorblind language to reflect goals and ideals that are antiracist and important to one's sense of self. This is important because, too often, researchers in the social sciences have buried the subjectivities of the people they study, blocking our ability to notice these distinctions and how they matter for individuals.

What might it look like, instead, to take them seriously? Doing so, after all, does not mean that we lose our ability to be critical of those identities and practices. Katharine

Tatum and Irene Browne (2016), for example, have made an effort to understand the distinction between a colorblind ideology and a colorblind identity, which they operationalize, following McDermott (2015) as a "personal disassociation from race" (3). They write, "We refer to the two together as a 'colour-blind approach.' Indeed, the two processes often function together" (ibid.). The disassociation element of their paradigm, of course, can be troublesome, as we know that disassociating from race does not make racism any less salient or real. No doubt this is a complicated and yet common dynamic, as Kettrey and Laster's (2014) research on online racism makes clear:

> In fact, we found that color-blind racism was so convincingly veiled that it was mistaken for dissent. This may have negative consequences for the destruction of racism online, as we found that users sometimes employed color-blind racism in an attempt to dissent against more blatant/overt racism. Relatedly, users also circulated color-blind racism in an attempt to support genuine dissent against racism. In both of these scenarios, users whom we label wannabe dissenters missed a valuable opportunity to critique racist attitudes that may maintain white privilege and, instead, they upheld the racial status quo. (270)

Even so, Hartmann et al. (2017) find that "Not only does colorblind identification not generate the same negative effects as measures of colorblind ideology, but it is also possible that a strong colorblind identification can have a positive effect on race relations" (882). Their work, therefore, helps us understand how colorblindness can work in a variety of ways, depending on the goals and identity (racial and otherwise) of the individual who is using this discourse and the context where it is applied.

This calls to mind Eileen O'Brien's (2000) research on white antiracist activists, where she found that

> Organizations that frame overt acts of racism as their main focus of activism and thus do not see themselves, as Whites,

as antagonists often use selective race cognizance. Under this way of thinking about race, one can use color and power evasive (colorblind) discourse about oneself and others, yet still be cognizant and vigilant about institutionalized racism in day to day life. (57)

She also says that this can function as "an antiracist way of thinking about race that incorporates elements of color-blindness and race cognizance in an effort to bridge the white divide" (58).

And yet, whiteness is not unique in this fashion. Vanessa Gonlin and Mary Campbell (2017) rightly point out that people of color have been understudied in prior examinations of colorblind ideology, and that closer attention to how distinct groups of people of color navigate colorblind frameworks alongside their racial and other identities is another important direction for new research. One such example is the work of Julie Dowling (2014), who proposes a racial ideology continuum for Mexican Americans, ranging from "whiteness" and colorblindness to identification as an antiracist racial "other." The existence of such a proposed continuum already breaks from the assumption that one's racial identity (in this case, as a Mexican American) will neatly map onto one's racial ideology (as colorblind or race-conscious). It also demonstrates the fluid nature, given the continuum, of such identities and ideologies – and therefore the diversity of thought and experience within any given racial group. Carefully tracing the emergence of these ideologies and identities alongside these experiences carries rich potential to tell us more about the contemporary racial landscape, both for people of color and as a whole. It is, again, the color-nuanced framework that O'Brien (2008) established, which was explored in the previous chapter.

Similarly, Katharine Tatum and Irene Browne's (2016) work on Dominican Americans in Atlanta explores how colorblindness may be utilized as a strategy to acculturate to, and cope with, US race relations. They are among several who are proposing an additional colorblind frame, theirs, which "illustrates the complexity of immigrant incorporation into the US" (21). They write, "Further, our results demonstrate how racial ideologies can be indeterminate and flexible at the level of individual identity while simultaneously upholding established racial hierarchies at the level of social organization" (21). The dynamics of colorblind racism among people of color illustrates and complicates Ashley "Woody" Doane's (2017) argument that ideologies are racist only to the degree that they maintain a racialized social system: that in and of themselves they are not racist. They are, instead, only one mechanism by which racism is practiced and advanced.

This allows us to consider the convergence of multiple ideologies that relate to race: that of colorblind racism and, for example, diversity ideology, which "assumes that race shapes individuals' worldviews and cultural practices, and that interaction across racial lines is positive and important" (Warikoo and de Novais 2014: 861). By examining students who add a diversity frame to a colorblind frame that they had developed often during high school, they find that "the colour-blind and diversity frames seem to co-occur in students' lives in ways that lead to ambivalence with respect to many race-related policies and racially marked experiences. [Their] findings suggest that contradictory race frames may reside within the same individual simultaneously, such that the individual draws upon one in some instances" (871). This emphasizes, they suggest, the role of institutions in shaping individuals' frames, as well as a less-recognized reality of how frames can overlap and come into conflict with one another.

Discussion Questions

- How does parsing colorblind ideology from colorblind identity help to provide further insight about the ways that people make sense of the social structures that surround them?
- To what extent does it seem that there may be a growing awareness of racism among the general public? What

might this tell us about contemporary racism and how it is best studied and addressed?

The White Elephant in the Room

There is a growing body of research into diversity frames, which Embrick (2011) suggests too often pays only lip service to diversity, without taking on the important work of altering the racial landscape to improve the experiences of people of color. My previous work (2012a, b) and new work by Candis Smith and Sarah Mayorga-Gallo (2017) suggest that diversity ideology allows whites to support principles of inclusion while failing to support policies or enact personal choices that adhere to these principles. Too often, instead, whites find ways to improve their own conditions or personal identities as "one of the good ones" (Burke 2017). These findings all suggest the need to deeply grapple with not just whiteness but the complex role of racial identities as they relate to ideology and discourse.

After all, the role of whites in antiracist efforts is a complicated one. Hughey (2012), for example, found a troubling pattern of white paternalism and a reliance on racist tropes even among a committed group of white antiracists. Somewhat similarly, my research in progressive Chicago communities showed a strong reliance on most frames of colorblind racism among whites who valued diversity in their communities (Burke 2012a), albeit in a somewhat distinct and still problematic "sympathetic" form (Burke 2018). All of this demonstrates how "racial dynamics are both deeply embedded but also malleable. Parents in [their] study come from backgrounds of white privilege. This history maintained a strong presence among [their] sample, yet we also saw race consciousness emerge" (Goar, Davis, and Manago 2017: 351). Kira Banks and I found the same to be true among students who undergo intensive antiracist training in a university setting (Burke and Banks 2012).

To complicate this, Apfelbaum, Sommers, and Norton (2008) have suggested that whites may deploy "strategic colorblindness: avoidance of talking about race – or even acknowledging racial difference – in an effort to avoid the appearance of bias" (918). They emphasize that people often are not colorblind at all – that they instead actively manage their expression of racial awareness depending on the context and their conversational partners. They write:

> We suspect that many individuals who exhibit colorblindness are not "racists" seeking to hide bias but rather relatively well-intentioned individuals who genuinely believe that colorblindness is a culturally sensitive approach to inter-group contact. Of course, the present findings indicate that this belief is often misplaced. Whites likely would be better served by employing alternative strategies, such as simply talking about race when it is clearly relevant or, more generally, engaging in affiliative behaviors in order to communicate positive interracial intentions. (930)

Of course, we know that positive intentions do not alone create a positive impact or outcome.

We also know, as Modica (2015) illustrates, that "racial identity among whites was infused with tensions over possible accusations of racism by African American students" (398). At the same time, "the possibility of being accused of racism was often connected to feelings of resentment and expressed with the 'reverse racism' discourse, wherein whites view themselves as the new victims of racial discrimination" (402). Even so, this attention to the realities of racial awareness and the role of context is an important new development in research into colorblind and contemporary racism.

This is especially true when considering social spaces where whites are the numerical minority. New research by Uma Jayakumar and Annie Adamain (2017) demon-strates that white students who attend historically black colleges and universities (HBCUs) behave in much the same way – demonstrating to others their awareness of racism that comes from their coursework and conversations, but also feeling victimized by these same discussions. Their white fragility (this intense perceived victimization and reaction thereto) tends to be more private, however, whereas their public presentation of self involves demonstrating to others that they are not individually complicit with systems and practices of racism, in part by displaying their "race cache," knowledge about racial matters and elements of racial subcultures, to others. On this basis, they, as have some others, suggest a potential fifth frame of colorblind discourse: the "disconnected power analysis" frame. These practices, again, are what help to create Smith and Mayorga-Gallo's (2017) "principle–policy gap."

This break from principles can also happen when racism is either being evaded, or willfully sidelined in order to preserve the racist status quo. One seemingly innocent way that this happens is through racial (and most often racist) humor. Sociologist Raúl Pérez has a growing body of research that explores the role of humor in colorblind and contemporary racism. His most recent article (2017) explores how comedians and other joke-tellers often deliberately situate their racist humor as an affront to political correctness, a move that illustrates a race-conscious rather than colorblind perspective.

At the same time, these same people often still deploy colorblind language by claiming to be "equal-opportunity offenders." And they do so, of course, in deeply unequal environments – such as in majority-white police forces where this form of humor is prevalent (ibid.). Dismissing such humor as "just jokes" flattens a sharply unequal racial landscape. It also attempts to forgive the perpetuation of the hateful and harmful notions that the attempted humor evokes by focusing on individual intentions rather than aggregate impact. It is a deep manifestation of "racism without racists" (Bonilla-Silva 2003).

It is also a kind of racial evasion – a term that Matthew Oware (2016) has given to practices that involve "(1) superficially referencing race, but not deliberately engaging or articulating racial dynamics, and (2) readily avoiding involved discussions surrounding racism occurring at the institutional or individual level that are quite obviously racial (through their history, construction, or manifestation)" (374). Evasion is not colorblindness, as racial contexts and expressions are deliberately set aside or actively ignored, such as, he suggests, in a race-neutral defense of the Confederate flag or, in his research, among white rappers who emphasize masculinity but ignore the important context of race and racism in hip-hop. In this sense, as Doane (2017) argues, "whites are not really 'color-blind,' they increasingly acknowledge and deliberately misrepresent the extent of systemic racism" (985). Future research must pay careful attention to how white people manage their knowledge of the realities of race and racism, rather than assuming that they do not. This is likely to reveal more knowledge about how racism is reproduced or challenged.

After all, we see many instances where, as Brooks et al. (2017) write, whites "claim victimization by government programs, college admissions policies, and employment hiring procedures that benefit people of color" (254). They write that while this is one mechanism that is commonly attributed to colorblind racism, "it diverges in an important way: in expressing their indignation, whites call attention to themselves as a persecuted ethnoracial group, rather than avoiding the subject of race" (ibid.). They call this white victimhood a distinct racial ideology, as it is neither colorblind nor overt/traditional. The fact that it can sit alongside other racial ideologies, they argue, simply reflects how "racial ideologies provide rhetorical tools designed to resonate with the structural, cultural, and political landscapes of a particular time. As such, ideologies often contradict one another" (256). This contradiction is far more of a puzzle for researchers wedded to their theoretical paradigms than they are for individuals who deploy them; individuals often do so simply out of ignorance or to further their personal goals. They may be far less concerned with ideological consistency than they are in preserving a sense of self that is likely to shift depending on their social contexts.

Ignorance is therefore also a sticky theoretical and scholarly subject, as it must weave together subjective knowledge and objective realities alongside intentions and impacts. Jennifer Mueller (2017) posits an "epistemology of ignorance" that structures white actors in an era of colorblindness and heightened racial awareness. She calls this epistemology of ignorance "a process of knowing designed to produce not knowing surrounding white privilege, culpability, and structural white supremacy" (220). She argues that a "singular structural focus may eclipse how whites use creative agency to reproduce, revise, and occasionally challenge white supremacy. Furthermore, these examples indirectly highlight an acknowledged but underexplored dimension of colorblindness; namely, rootedness in ignorance" (221).

Focusing on how students who had learned about historical, institutional, and ideological processes of racism managed this knowledge, she identifies four dominant practices: "(1) evading; (2) willfully reasoning colorblindness; (3) tautologically reasoning ignorance; and (4) mystifying practical solutions" (225).

All of these attribute agency to those who deny racism. But as Mueller writes:

> Most work appears to assume whites are only creatively agentic when they resist white supremacy. While resisting one's possessive investment in whiteness is certainly the path of greater resistance, we should not discount how agency and innovation influence more conservative reproduction as well. Nor should we assume whites' racial consciousness is inevitably antiracist and will embolden countervailing praxis. Examining colorblindness as an everyday, recursive accomplishment brings these nuances into relief. (2017: 234)

Ongoing attention to the practices of racial consciousness and evasion will reveal the question of *how*, rather than *whether*, those who can protect racial advantages may act to do so. Given that self-preservation for whites in a racist society is rarely challenging, this will almost always happen at the expense of people of color. Noticing and challenging this resistance to the realities of racism, rather than to racism itself, can provide points of leverage to potentially alter those systems toward greater equity.

Discussion Questions

• Why is a sharp focus on whiteness and the practices that uphold it necessary when examining challenges to and changes surrounding contemporary racism?
• What are some ways that whites can understand the realities of racism and act to support racial justice efforts?

Challenging Contemporary Racism

Much of the research above, and more that is surely to follow, demonstrates ways in which race is not being ignored, in a typical colorblind fashion, but rather being claimed and/or co-opted. This can be an active negotiation with the realities of race and racism, rather than sheer ignorance toward or denial of those realities. Recent social movements from Black Lives Matter to the emboldening of white supremacists in and connected to the alt right are making the salience of race and discussions of racism ever more prominent in public life. As such, continuing attention to the ways that people, both ordinary and powerful, make use of an increasing awareness of racism will surely reveal new insights about the workings of our racialized social system more broadly. This research has the potential to show us what people actually do with the things that they know, or think they know, about race and racism, and how that knowledge informs practices that may either transform or sustain the racist status quo.

This research also helps us to appreciate the contextual nature of colorblind discourses and ideologies, and the subjectivities of those who enact them. This is, again, important in the examination of how people of color, who are subject to the negative consequences of racism, make use of colorblind and other frameworks to navigate a racist society in ways that will necessarily differ from those of whites whose racial privileges can sustain blindness to the realities of racism. This helps us to see the fluid and contingent nature of ideological and discursive systems. This is an important new strain of research, as it breaks from some prior assumptions that colorblindness is always only about a defense of racism or a reflection of ignorance. It also forces us to pay attention to how ideologies are deployed in connection to the real-world institutions and power relations that create racial inequalities. After all, paying attention to the dynamics between self and society in close connection to the contexts where that dynamic is played out is the best way to understand fully how systems of racism operate and may be challenged.

This question of how institutions and ideologies can be challenged is, unfortunately, one of the least studied terrains of study in sociology broadly, and in the study of racism specifically. But greater attention to the changing dynamics of racism will provide better opportunities to examine this than would continuing to work with the assumption that colorblindness is either the sole, or an otherwise unchanging, element of contemporary racism. Further, it seems clear that more and more people are aware of the realities of racism, and are willing to acknowledge and discuss them than might have ever been imaginable even as recently as in the early years of the Obama presidency, where the dominant discourse (much to the dismay of social scientists) was one of an (imagined) post-racial United States. It seems reasonable, then, that even when colorblindness is deployed, it is not done with uniform intent:

> "Colorblindness" may be little more than a form of antiracism "lite," but the fact that millions of whites (and not only whites) identify with this idea, and the fact that many whites have adopted a more serious antiracism – many students for example, cultural workers, "movement people," etc., who cannot be dismissed as mere tokens or exceptions – clearly calls into question the rigidities of [some previous analyses]. (Omi and Winant 2015: 123)

It also reflects the potential for changing racial dynamics in the USA.

Woody Doane's (2017) recent work re-emphasizes the plurality of racial ideologies, "collections of beliefs and understandings about race and the role of race in social interaction," (976) and asserts that ideologies are only racist to the extent that they help to support a racialized social system. Colorblindness should not be, he says, always conflated with prejudice but rather considered alongside tangible social realities. Research about people of color and the ways that they negotiate racial ideologies alongside racist realities are only one of the strains of scholarship that make this clear.

As I (Burke 2016), Bonilla-Silva (2015), and others have suggested, we must also continually trace our examinations of colorblind ideology and discourse so that we remain centered on the material realities (outcomes, disparities, experiences, and more) that specific institutions and social settings help to create alongside them. This also helps us to appreciate – as, again, Doane (2017) suggests is crucial – how colorblindness is always a process, one always morphing and changing in relation to the settings where it is being utilized. This can, as part of this discussion has emphasized, include antiracist or progressive initiatives. It is for this reason that those who are seeking to talk about race, no matter how clumsily, and to make change, no matter how imperfect, should also be the focus of future studies. An insight into their realities, their ways of thinking and talking, and the ongoing challenges and resistance they encounter, will surely reveal more about the intricate workings of a racist society and provide direct cues about how it can be improved.

This will necessarily involve a deeper consideration of intersectionality than many previous studies have engaged. Angie Beeman's (2015) study of social movement organizing activity suggests that "placing gender and racial oppression explicitly rather than implicitly at the center of the organiza-tion's agenda along with class oppression may better enable any group to dismantle larger systems of oppression" (145).

Hagerman (2016) similarly suggests the need to acknowledge the agency of children and the potential that they bring to alter the status quo. And, as movements from Civil Rights to Black Lives Matter demonstrate, queer organizers are often central to the success of these movements, likely given the intersectional lens that their lived experience may generate.

And so, how do we effectively challenge new forms of racism, and ensure that a *new* "new racism" does not take its place? While Bonilla-Silva is cynical about education and urges systemic changes to overcome systemic racism (see 1996: 476), it remains true that acknowledging the existence of a problem is a vital first step toward addressing it. This is, of course, a direct affront to colorblindness: more of us need to be willing to see, acknowledge, and not evade the realities of racism and racial inequalities in our societies. We must challenge the forms of colorblindness that practice Mueller's (2017) epistemology of ignorance and instead join forces with those who practice colorblindness as an ideal (Hartmann et al. 2017) and those who engage antiracism as a practice.

Antiracism as a practice must always attend to the material realities of racial violence and racial inequality, and center itself on improving the conditions for those who are marginalized by our racialized social systems. While ideologies help to buttress or challenge those systems, at the end of the day, it is our daily and nightly practices and the associated landscape of opportunities that must fundamentally change if we want to create institutions and interactions that live up to colorblind ideals. This is necessarily a multi-pronged approach, as the volumes of research on contemporary racism demonstrate that colorblind and other racisms have permeated nearly every social, political, and institutional space. As such, it is in those myriad spaces where practices that perpetuate inequality and violence (including symbolic violence) must be actively altered.

There is no magic formula for how racism, as a widespread practice and lived reality, can be altered. But it is also no secret. We simply must insist that things change – in our

families, in our friendship circles, in our schools and neighborhoods, in our governmental and workplace policies and
practices, and more. Often the research is quite clear about
where the problems lie; we must continue this research and
also trust those who experience the violence of racism to
know when and where these acts (or inactions, or silences)
are taking place. And then we must focus on those spaces to
bring about necessary change.

We can anticipate resistance to that change – there always
is. The logic and discourse of that resistance is likely to
reproduce colorblind racist beliefs. But those beliefs can
and should be challenged – this becomes the moment for
active persuasion through logic, evidence, and appeals to
our shared humanity. And given that these debates will not
be abstract, but rather tied to specific changes that are being
proposed, they can remain tangible while also appealing to
colorblind ideals – that race should not matter (and as such,
racially disparate practices can and should be eradicated).
In these ways ideologies are not disconnected from their
material roots, but are rather strategies that can and should
be used to negotiate changing practices and their impact on
our real lives. Given that few people explicitly want racism
and racial inequalities, this creates a fissure – an opportunity
to break with the status quo and actively create new ways of
doing things. These, too, will generate new ways of making
sense of the world, and help to spread alternative antiracist
ideologies and practices.

It is likely that I am making things sound too simple. But
the reality is that too often we run from those debates over
real problems in our actual communities or organizations,
and instead favor ideological echo chambers where we speak
only with those who already agree with us and fight the
monsters of racism "out there" rather than in our intimate
lives and shared communities. When we work on our own
spheres of influence, and leverage the power that we all have,
albeit to varying degrees given the realities of multiple layers
of inequalities, we can and must work to make not just the
world, but our own specific worlds, better places. This is the

only way we can move out of a cynical or passive state and into opportunities for real change and growth.

Further Exploration

• Develop research questions that further antiracism efforts by carefully studying the complex dynamics of contemporary, colorblind racism.
• We all have differing spheres of influence in our friend circles, spiritual or religious communities, neighborhoods, workplaces, and more. Make a list of at least three tangible things that you could do to create more racial justice in those spaces. Put this list someplace you will see it, until you have helped to implement these practices. Then, start again. Remember to keep people of color and their insights at the center of these efforts, without asking them to shoulder a disproportionate share of the work.

Appendix: Scholarly Timeline

1970   Joel Kovel named the "aversive" racist as "the type who believes in white race superiority but does nothing overt about it" (54).

1973   Sears and McConahay write that symbolic racism involves "abstract moral assertions about blacks' behavior as a group, concerning what blacks deserve, how they ought to act, whether or not they are treated equitably, and so on" (138–9).

1976   McConahay and Hough defined "symbolic racism" as "the expression in terms of abstract ideological symbols and symbolic behaviors of the feeling that blacks are violating cherished values and making illegitimate demands for changes in the racial status quo" (38).

1979   Pettigrew terms a "new" racism – a term that political scientists Sniderman et al. (1991) operationalize as covert and symbolic – though Pettigrew would again call it "modern" racism in 1989.

1981   Sears and Kinder define symbolic racism as a "blend of antiblack affect and the kind of traditional American moral values embodied in the Protestant Ethic" (416).

1983   McConahay advances a theory of "modern racism"

for which he, with colleagues, had also developed a scale (McConahay, Hardee, and Batts 1981). They write, "Previous work with the concept of modern racism has termed it 'symbolic racism'.... The label was changed from symbolic to modern racism in order to emphasize the contemporary, post Civil Rights Movement nature of the beliefs and issues" (1981: 564–5).

1984 Mary Jackman and Michael Muha argue that ideologies are more important than attitudes relative to this new racism.

1993 Ruth Frankenburg discusses colorblind racism in her study of white women and race/racism, where she prefers a framework of "color evasiveness" and "power evasiveness."

1995 Pettigrew, with his colleague Meertens, discusses "subtle" racism, emphasizing its covert rather than blatant nature, and writing that it is "cool, distant, indirect" (1995: 58).

1995 Robert C. Smith, in 1995, wrote *Racism in the Post-Civil Rights Era: Now You See It, Now You Don't.*

1997 Leslie G. Carr's (1997) book *"Color-Blind" Racism* is published, as is journalist Ellis Cose's book *Color-Blind: Seeing Beyond Race in a Race-Obsessed World.*

1997 Lawrence Bobo, James R. Kluegel, and Ryan A. Smith develop a term called *laissez-faire* racism, which "involves persistent negative stereotyping of African Americans, a tendency to blame blacks themselves for the black–white gap in socioeconomic standing, and resistance to meaningful policy efforts to ameliorate US racist social conditions and institutions" (16).

2000 Helen Neville and colleagues develop the Colorblind Racial Attitudes Scale (CoBRAS).

2000 Bonilla-Silva and Forman explore the rhetorical strategies "that allow [whites] to safely voice racial views that might be otherwise interpreted as racist" (68–9).

2000 Eileen O'Brien publishes "Are We Supposed to be Colorblind or Not? Competing Frames Used by Whites Against Racism." *Race and Society* 3(1): 41–59.

2003 Eduardo Bonilla-Silva publishes *Racism Without Racists: Color-Blind Racism and the Persistence of Racial Inequality in the United States;* Michael K. Brown, Martin Carnoy, Troy Duster, and David B. Oppenheimer publish *Whitewashing Race: The Myth of a Color-Blind Society.* Charles Gallagher also publishes an article about colorblind racism.

References

Alegria, Sharla. 2014. "Constructing Racial Difference Through Group Talk: An Analysis of White Focus Groups' Discussion of Racial Profiling." *Ethnic and Racial Studies* 37(2): 241–60.

Alexander, Michelle. 2010. *The New Jim Crow: Mass Incarceration in the Age of Colorblindness.* New York: The New Press.

Anderson, Bridget 2001. "Just Another Job? Paying for Domestic Work." *Gender and Development* 9(1): 25–33.

Anderson, Elijah. 2011. *The Cosmopolitan Canopy: Race and Civility in Everyday Life.* New York: W. W. Norton and Company.

Anderson, Michelle Wilde. 2004. "Colorblind Segregation: Equal Protection as a Bar to Neighborhood Integration." *California Law Review* 92: 841–4.

Apfelbaum, Evan P., Samuel R. Sommers, and Michael I. Norton. 2008. "Seeing Race and Seeming Racist? Evaluating Strategic Colorblindness in Social Interaction." *Journal of Personality and Social Psychology* 95(4): 918–32.

Bader, Michael D. M. and Maria Krysan. 2015. "Community Attraction and Avoidance in Chicago: What's Race Got to Do With It?" *Annals of the American Academy of Political and Social Science* 660(1): 261–81.

Baldwin, Bridgette. 2009. "Colorblind Diversity: The Changing Significance of "Race" in the Post-Bakke Era." *Albany Law Review* 72: 863–90.

Banales, Josefina. 2014. "The Sustained Impact of an Engaging

Diversity Program on College Seniors' Color-Blind Racial Attitudes." *CrissCross* 2(1): 1.

Barber, Kendra Hadiya. 2011. "'What Happened to All the Protests?' Black Megachurches' Responses to Racism in a Colorblind Era." *Journal of African American Studies* 15(2): 218–35.

Barr, Simone C. and Helen A. Neville. 2014. "Racial Socialization, Color-Blind Racial Ideology, and Mental Health among Black College Students: An Examination of an Ecological Model." *Journal of Black Psychology* 40(2): 138–65.

Basler, Carleen. 2008. "White Dreams and Red Votes: Mexican Americans and the Lure of Inclusion in the Republican Party." *Ethnic and Racial Studies* 31(1): 123–66.

Beeman, Angie. 2015. "Walk the Walk but Don't Talk the Talk: The Strategic Use of Color-Blind Ideology in an Interracial Social Movement Organization." *Sociological Forum* 30(1): 127–47.

Bell, Joyce M. and Douglas Hartmann. 2007. "Diversity in Everyday Discourse: The Cultural Ambiguities and Consequences of "Happy Talk." *American Sociological Review* 72: 895–914.

Berry, Brent and Eduardo Bonilla-Silva. 2008. "They Should Hire the One With the Best Score': White Sensitivity to Qualification Differences in Affirmative Action Hiring Decisions." *Ethnic and Racial Studies* 31: 215–42.

Bimper Jr., Albert Y. 2015. "Lifting the Veil: Exploring Colorblind Racism in Black Student Athlete Experiences." *Journal of Sport and Social Issues* 39(3): 225–43.

Blauner, Robert. 1972. *Racial Oppression in America*. New York: Harper Collins.

Bobo, Lawrence D., James R. Kluegel, and Ryan A. Smith. 1997. "Laissez-Faire Racism: The Crystallization of a Kinder, Gentler, Antiblack Ideology." *Racial Attitudes in the 1990s: Continuity and Change* 15: 23–5.

Bobo, Lawrence D., Camille Z. Charles, Maria Krysan, Alicia D. Simmons, and George M. Fredrickson. 2012. "The Real Record on Racial Attitudes." *Social Trends in American Life: Findings from the General Social Survey since 1972*: 38–83.

Boddie, Elise C. 2015. "Critical Mass and the Paradox of Colorblind Individualism in Equal Protection." *University of Pennsylvania Journal of Constitutional Law* 17(3): 781–818.

Bonilla-Silva, Eduardo. 1997. "Rethinking Racism: Toward A Structural Interpretation." *American Sociological Review*: 465–80.

———— 2001. *White Supremacy and Racism in the Post-Civil Rights Era*. Boulder, CO: Lynne Rienner.

———— 2003/ 2006. *Racism without Racists: Color-Blind Racism and the Persistence of Racial Inequality in the United States*. Rowman & Littlefield.

———— 2015. "More than Prejudice: Restatement, Reflections, and New Directions in Critical Race Theory." *Sociology of Race and Ethnicity* 1(1): 73–87.

Bonilla-Silva, Eduardo and Tyrone A. Forman. 2000. "'I Am Not a Racist But ...': Mapping White College Students' Racial Ideology in the USA." *Discourse and Society* 11(1): 50–85.

Bonilla-Silva, Eduardo, Amanda Lewis, and David G. Embrick. 2004. "'I Did Not Get That Job Because of A Black Man ...': The Story Lines and Testimonies of Color-Blind Racism." *Sociological Forum* 19: 555–81.

Bonilla-Silva, Eduardo and David G. Embrick. 2007. "'Every Place Has a Ghetto ...': The Significance of Whites' Social and Residential Segregation." *Symbolic Interaction* 30(3): 323–45.

Bonilla-Silva, Eduardo and David Dietrich. 2011. "The Sweet Enchantment of Color-Blind Racism in Obamerica." *Annals of the American Academy of Political and Social Science* 634: 190–206.

Brodkin, Karen. 1998. *How Jews Became White Folks and What that says about Race in America*. New Brunswick, NJ: Rutgers University Press.

Brooks, Erinn, Kim Ebert, and Tyler Flockhart. 2017. "Examining the Reach of Color Blindness: Ideological Flexibility, Frame Alignment, and Legitimacy among Racially Conservative and Extremist Organizations." *Sociological Quarterly* 58(2): 254–76.

Brown, Amy. 2013. "Waiting for Superwoman: White Female Teachers and the Construction of the 'Neoliberal Savior' in a New York City Public School." *Journal for Critical Education Policy Studies (JCEPS)* 11(2): 123–64.

Brown, Frank. 2004. "Nixon's" southern strategy" and forces against Brown." *Journal of Negro Education* July: 191–208.

Brown, Michael K., Martin Carnoy, Troy Duster, and David B. Oppenheimer. 2003. *Whitewashing Race: The Myth of a Color-Blind Society*. Berkeley: University of California Press.

Burke, Meghan A. 2012a. *Racial Ambivalence in Diverse Communities: Whiteness and the Power of Colorblind Ideologies*. Lanham, PA: Lexington Books.

———— 2012b. "Discursive Fault Lines: Reproducing White Habitus in a Racially Diverse Community." *Critical Sociology*. 38(5): 645–68.

———— 2015. *Race, Gender, and Class in the Tea Party: What the Movement Reflects about Mainstream Ideologies*. Lanham, PA: Lexington Books.

———— 2016. "New Frontiers in the Study of Colorblind Racism: A Materialist Approach." *Social Currents* 3(2): 103–9.

———— 2017. "Racing Left and Right: Colorblind Racism's Dominance Across the US Political Spectrum." *Sociological Quarterly*, 58(2): 277–94.

———— 2018. "Sympathetic Racism: Color-Blind Racism's Liberal Flair in Three Chicago Neighborhoods," chapter under contract for *Challenging the Status Quo: Diversity, Democracy, and Equality in the 21st Century*, ed. Sharon Collins and David G. Embrick.

Burke, Meghan A. and Kira Hudson Banks. 2012. "Sociology by Any Other Name: Teaching the Sociological Perspective in Campus Diversity Programs." *Teaching Sociology* 40(1): 21–3.

Cabrera, Nolan L. 2014a. "'But I'm Oppressed Too': White Male College Students Framing Racial Emotions as Facts and Recreating Racism." *International Journal of Qualitative Studies in Education* 27(6): 768–84.

———— 2014b. "But We're Not Laughing: White Male College Students' Racial Joking and What This Says About" Post-Racial" Discourse." *Journal of College Student Development* 55(1): 1–15.

Callahan, Nicole Soojung. 2014. "Conclusion: Talking About Race and Adoption," pp. 242–7 in *Race in Transnational and Transracial Adoption*, ed. Vilna Treitler. New York: Palgrave McMillan.

Callero, Peter L. 2013. *The Myth of Individualism: How Social Forces Shape Our Lives*. Lanham, PA: Rowman & Littlefield.

Campón, Rebecca Rangel and Robert T. Carter. 2015. "The Appropriated Racial Oppression Scale: Development and Preliminary Validation." *Cultural Diversity and Ethnic Minority Psychology* 21(4): 497–506.

Carr, Leslie G. 1997. *"Color-Blind" Racism*. Thousand Oaks: Sage Publications.

Castagno, Angelina E. 2013. "Multicultural Education and the Protection of Whiteness." *American Journal of Education* 120: 101–28.

Chapman, Thandeka K. 2013. "You Can't Erase Race! Using CRT to Explain the Presence of Race and Racism in Majority White Suburban Schools." *Discourse: Studies in the Cultural Politics of Education* 34(4): 611–27.

Chen, Grace A., Paul LePhuoc, Michele R. Guzmán, Stephanie S. Rude, and Barbara G. Dodd. 2006. "Exploring Asian American Racial Identity." *Cultural Diversity and Ethnic Minority Psychology* 12(3): 461–76.

Childs, Erica Chito. 2006. "Black and White: Family Opposition to Becoming Multiracial," pp. 233–46 in *Mixed Messages: Multiracial Identities in the "Color-Blind" Era*, ed. David L. Brunsma. Boulder, CO: Lynne Rienner.

Chiswick, Barry R. and Noyna DebBurman. 2004. "Educational Attainment: Analysis by Immigrant Generation." *Economics of Education Review* 23(4): 361–79.

Chomsky, Aviva. 2007. *They Take Our Jobs!: And 20 Other Myths About Immigration*. Boston: Beacon Press.

Cleland, Jamie., 2013. "Racism, Football Fans, and Online Message Boards: How Social Media has added a New Dimension to Racist Discourse in English Football." *Journal of Sport and Social Issues* 38 5): 415–31.

Cobb, Ryon J., Samuel L. Perry, and Kevin D. Dougherty. 2015. "United by faith? Race/ethnicity, Congregational Diversity, and Explanations of Racial Inequality." *Sociology of Religion* 76(2): 177–98.

Coleman, M. Nicole, Stephanie Chapman, and David C. Wang. 2012. "An Examination of Color-Blind Racism and Race-Related Stress among African American Undergraduate students." *Journal of Black Psychology* 39(5): 486–504.

Cooper, Anna Julia. [1892] 1988. *A Voice From the South*. New York: Oxford University Press.

Cose, Ellis. 1997. *Color-Blind: Seeing Beyond Race in a Race-Obsessed World*. New York: HarperCollins.

Crenshaw, Kimberlé. 1991. "Mapping the Margins: Intersectionality, Identity Politics, and Violence against Women of Color." *Stanford Law Review* 43(6): 1241–99.

——— 1998. "Colorblind Rhetoric." *The Southern Communication Journal* 63(3): 244–56.

Crespino, Joseph. 2007. *In Search of Another Country: Mississippi and the Conservative Counterrevolution*. Princeton University Press.

Croll, Paul R. 2013. "Explanations for Racial Disadvantage and Racial Advantage: Beliefs about Both Sides of Inequality in America." *Ethnic and Racial Studies* 36: 47–74.

Daniels, Jessie. 2009a. *Cyber Racism: White Supremacy Online and the New Attack on Civil Rights*. Lanham, PA: Rowman & Littlefield.

——— 2009b. "Cloaked Websites: Propaganda, Cyber-Racism and Epistemology in the Digital Era." *New Media and Society* 11(5): 659–83.

——— 2013. "Race and Racism in Internet Studies: A Review and Critique." *New Media and Society* 15(5): 695–719.

Daniels, Jessie and Nick Lalone. 2012. "Racism in Video Gaming: Connecting Extremist and Mainstream Expressions of White Supremacy," pp. 85–99 in *Social Exclusion, Power, and Video Game Play: New Research in Digital Media and Eechnology*, eds. David G. Embrick, J. Talmadge Wright, and Andras Lukacs. Lanham, PA: Lexington Press.

Darling, Marsha and Jean Tyson. 2001. *Race, Voting, Redistricting, and the Constitution: Sources and Explorations on the Fifteenth Amendment*. Vol. 1. New York: Routledge.

DeFreece, Alfred W. 2014. "When the R Word Ain't Enough: Exploring Black Youths' Structural Explanations of Black Group Status." *Humanity and Society* 38: 25–48.

de Leon, Cedric. 2011. "Emerald Book Chapter: The More Things Change: A Gramscian Genealogy of Barack Obama's" Post-Racial" Politics, 1932–2008." *Political Power and Social Theory* 22: 75–104.

Desmond, Matthew. 2016. *Evicted: Poverty and Profit in an American City*. New York: Crown.

Doane, Woody. 2017. "Beyond Color-blindness: (Re) Theorizing Racial Ideology." *Sociological Perspectives* 60(5): 975–991.

Douglas, Karen Manges, Rogelio Sáenz, and Aurelia Lorena Murga. 2015. *American Behavioral Scientist* 59(11): 1429–1451

Dowling, Julie A. 2014. *Mexican Americans and the Question of Race*. Austin, TX: University of Texas Press.

Embrick, David G. 2011. "The Diversity Ideology in the Business World: A New Oppression for a New Age." *Critical Sociology* 37(5): 541–56.

Embrick, David G. and Kasey Henricks. 2013. "Discursive Colorlines at Work: How Epithets and Stereotypes are Racially Unequal." *Symbolic Interaction* 36(2): 197–215.

Ernst, Rose. 2010. *The Price of Progressive Politics: The Welfare Rights Movement in an Era of Colorblind Racism.* New York: NYU Press.

Feagin, Joe R. 2012. *White Party, White Government: Race, Class, and US Politics.* New York: Routledge.

—— [2006] 2013. *Systemic Racism: A Theory of Oppression.* New York: Routledge.

—— 2014. *Racist America: Roots, Current Realities, and Future Reparations.* New York: Routledge.

Feagin, Joe R. and Sean Elias. 2013. "Rethinking Racial Formation Theory: A Systemic Racism Critique." *Ethnic and Racial Studies* 36(6): 931–60.

Forman, Tyrone A. 2004. "Color-Blind Racism and Racial Indifference: The Role of Racial Apathy in Facilitating Enduring Inequalities." In *the Changing Terrain of Race and Ethnicity*, eds. Maria Krysan and Amanda Lewis. New York: Russell Sage Foundation.

Frankenberg, Ruth. 1993. *White Women, Race Matters.* Minneapolis, MN: University of Minnesota Press.

Freeman, Eric. 2005. "No Child Left Behind and the Denigration of Race." *Equity and Excellence in Education* 38: 190–9.

Frymer, Paul. 2008. *Black and Blue: African Americans, the Labor Movement, and the Decline of the Democratic Party.* Princeton University Press.

Gallagher, Charles A. 2003. "Color-Blind Privilege: The Social and Political Functions of Erasing the Color Line in Post Race America." *Race, Gender and Class* 10: 22–37.

Gans, Herbert. J. 1995. *The War Against the Poor: The Underclass and Antipoverty Policy.* New York: Basic Books.

George, Hermon. 2013. "Neoliberalism in Blackface: Barack Obama and Deracialization, 2007–2012." *Journal of Pan African Studies* 6(6): 240–77.

Goar, Carla. 2014. "Culture at Camp: White Parents' Understanding of Race," pp. 190–203 in *Race in Transnational and Transracial Adoption*, ed. Vilna Treitler. New York: Palgrave McMillan.

Goar, Carla, Jenny L. Davis, and Bianca Manago. 2017. "Discursive Entwinement: How White Transracially Adoptive

Parents Navigate Race." *Sociology of Race and Ethnicity* 3(3): 338–54.

Godfrey, Erin B. and Sharon Wolf. 2016. "Developing Critical Consciousness or Justifying the System? A Qualitative Analysis of Attributions for Poverty and Wealth among Low-Income Racial/Ethnic Minority and Immigrant Women." *Cultural Diversity and Ethnic Minority Psychology* 22(1): 93–103.

Goldberg, David Theo. 2009. *Threat of Race: Reflections on Racial Neoliberalism.* Hoboken, New Jersey: John Wiley & Sons.

Gonlin, Vanessa and Mary E. Campbell. 2017. "Is Blindness Contagious? Examining Racial Attitudes among People of Color with Close Interracial Relationships." *Sociological Perspectives* 60(5): 937–55.

Gonzalez Van Cleve, Nicole and Lauren Mayes. 2015. "Criminal Justice Through 'Colorblind' Lenses: A Call to Examine the Mutual Constitution of Race and Criminal Justice." *Law and Social Inquiry* 40(2): 406–32.

Gotanda, Neil. 1995. "A Critique of 'Our Constitution is Colorblind,'" pp. 257–75 in *Critical Race Theory: The Key Writings that Formed the Movement*, eds. Kimberlé Crenshaw, Neil Gotanda, Gary Peller, and Kendall Thomas. New York: The New Press.

Gottlieb, Dylan. 2013. "Sixth Avenue Heartache: Race, Commemoration, and the Colorblind Consensus in Zephyrhills, Florida, 2003–2004." *Journal of Urban History* 39: 1085–105.

Hachfield, Axinja, Adam Hahn, Sascha Schroeder, Yvonne Anders, and Mereike Kunter. 2015. "Should Teachers Be Colorblind? How Multicultural and Egalitarian Beliefs Differentially Relate to Aspects of Teachers' Professional Competence for Teaching in Diverse Classrooms." *Teaching and Teacher Education* 48: 44–55.

Hagerman, Margaret Ann. 2016. "Reproducing and Reworking Colorblind Racial Ideology: Acknowledging Children's Agency in the White Habitus." *Sociology of Race and Ethnicity* 2(1): 58–71.

Harper, Shaun R. 2012. "Race without Racism: How Higher Education Researchers Minimize Racist Institutional Norms." *Review of Higher Education* 36(1): 9–29.

Harris Combs, Barbara. 2016. "Black (and Brown) Bodies Out of

Place: Towards a Theoretical Understanding of Systematic Voter Suppression in the United States." *Critical Sociology* 42(4–5): 535–49.

Hartmann, Douglas, Paul R. Croll, Ryan Larson, Joseph Gerteis, and Alex Manning. 2017. "Colorblindness as Identity: Key Determinants, Relations to Ideology, and Implications for Attitudes about Race and Policy." *Sociological Perspectives* 60(5): 866–88.

Hawkins, Nick. 2015. "Hate Crime in Sport," p. 327 in *The Routledge International Handbook on Hate Crime*, eds. Nathan Hall, Abbee Corb, Paul Giannasi, and John G. D. Grieve. London: Routledge.

Hill, Jane H. 2008. *The Everyday Language of White Racism*. Oxford, UK: John Wiley & Sons.

Hughey, Matthew W. 2011. "Backstage Discourse and the Reproduction of White Masculinities." *Sociological Quarterly* 52: 132–53.

—— 2012. *White Bound: Nationalists, Antiracists, and the Shared Meanings of Race*. Redwood City, CA: Stanford University Press.

Hunt, Matthew O. 2007. "African American, Hispanic, and White Beliefs about Black/White Inequality, 1977–2004." *American Sociological Review* 72(3): 390–415.

Inwood, Joshua F. J. 2015. "Neoliberal Racism: The 'Southern Strategy' and the Expanding Geographies of White Supremacy." *Social and Cultural Geography* 16(4): 407–23.

Jackman, Mary R. and Michael J. Muha. 1984. "Education and Intergroup Attitudes: Moral Enlightenment, Superficial Democratic Commitment, or Ideological Refinement?" *American Sociological Review* 49(6): 751–69.

Jansen, Wiebren S., Menno W. Vos, Sabine Otten, Astrid Podsiadlowski, and Karen I. van der Zee. 2016. "Colorblind or Colorful? How Diversity Approaches Affect Cultural Majority and Minority Employees." *Journal of Applied Social Psychology* 46(2): 81–93.

Jayakumar, Uma M. 2015. "The Shaping of Postcollege Colorblind Orientation Among Whites: Residential Segregation and Campus Diversity Experiences." *Harvard Educational Review* 85(4): 609–45.

Jayakumar, Uma M. and Annie S. Adamain. 2017. "The Fifth Frame of Colorblind Ideology: Maintaining the Comforts of

Colorblindness in the Context of White Fragility." *Sociological Perspectives* 60(5): 912–36.

Johnson, Heather Beth. 2014. *The American Dream and the Power of Wealth: Choosing Schools and Inheriting Inequality in the Land of Opportunity*. New York: Routledge.

Joseph, Nicole M., Kara Mitchell Viesca, and Margarita Bianco. 2016. "Black Female Adolescents and Racism in Schools: Experiences in a Colorblind Society." *The High School Journal* 100(1): 4–25.

Kao, Grace and Kara Joyner. 2004. "Do Race and Ethnicity Matter among Friends? Activities among Interracial, Interethnic, and Intraethnic Adolescent Friends." *Sociological Quarterly* 45(3): 557–73.

Katz, Michael B. [1989] 2013. *The Undeserving Poor: America's Enduring Confrontation with Poverty: Fully Updated and Revised*. New York: Oxford University Press.

Kettrey, Heather Hensman and Whitney Nicole Laster. 2014. "Staking Territory in the 'World White Web': an Exploration of the Roles of Overt and Color-Blind Racism in Maintaining Racial Boundaries on a Popular Web Site." *Social Currents* 1(3): 257–74.

Kinder, Donald R. and David O. Sears. 1981. "Prejudice and Politics: Symbolic Racism versus Racial Threats to the Good Life." *Journal of Personality and Social Psychology* 40(3): 414.

King, C. Richard and David J. Leonard. 2014. *Beyond Hate: White Power and Popular Culture*. Surrey: Ashgate Publishing Group.

Korgen, Kathleen Odell. 2009. "Black/White Biracial Identity: The Influence of Colorblindness and the Racialization of Poor Black Americans." *Theory in Action* 2: 23–39.

Korgen, Kathleen Odell and Eileen O'Brien. 2006. "Black/White Friendships in a Color-Blind Society," pp. 267–84 in *Mixed Messages: Multiracial Identities in the "Color-Blind" Era*, ed. David L. Brunsma. Boulder, CO: Lynne Rienner.

Korver-Glenn, Elizabeth. 2014. "Color-Blind Racism among Non-poor Latinos in a Redeveloping Houston Barrio." MA Thesis, Rice University.

Kovel, Joel. 1970. *White Racism: A Psychohistory*. New York: Pantheon.

Lassiter, Matthew D. 2006. *The Silent Majority: Suburban Politics in the Sunbelt South*. Princeton University Press.

Lawson, Steven F. 2011. "Long Origins of the Short Civil Rights

Movement, 1954–1968." pp. 9–37 in *Freedom Rights: New Perspectives on the Civil Rights Movement*, ed. Danielle L. McGuire and John Dittmer. University Press of Kentucky.

Léonard, Marie des Neiges. 2014. "Census and Racial Categorization in France: Invisible Categories and Color-Blind Politics." *Humanity and Society* 38(1): 67–88.

Leonardo, Zeus and Michalinos Zembylas. 2013. "Whiteness as Technology of Affect: Implications for Educational Praxis." *Equity and Excellence in Education* 46(1): 150–65.

Lewis, Amanda E., Mark Chesler, and Tyrone A. Forman. 2000. "The Impact of 'Colorblind' Ideologies on Students of Color: Intergroup Relations at a Predominantly White University." *Journal of Negro Education* 69: 74–91.

López, Ian F. Haney. 2007. "'A Nation of Minorities': Race, Ethnicity, and Reactionary Colorblindness." *Stanford Law Review* 59: 985–1063.

—— 2014. *Dog Whistle Politics: How Coded Racial Appeals Have Reinvented Racism and Wrecked the Middle Class*. New York: Oxford University Press.

McAdam, Doug. 1999. *Political Process and the Development of Black Insurgency, 1930–1970*. Chicago: University of Chicago Press.

McClain, Paula D., Niambi M. Carter, Victoria M. DeFrancesco Soto, Monique L. Lyle, Jeffrey D. Grynaviski, Shayla C. Nunnally, Thomas J. Scotto, J. Alan Kendrick, Gerald F. Lackey, and Kendra Davenport Cotton. 2006. "Racial Distancing in a Southern City: Latino Immigrants' Views of Black Americans." *Journal of Politics* 68(3): 571–84.

MacLean, Nancy, 2008. *Freedom Is Not Enough: The Opening of the American Workplace*. Cambridge, MA: Harvard University Press.

McConahay, John B. 1983. "Modern Racism and Modern Discrimination: The Effects of Race, Racial Attitudes, and Context on Simulated Hiring Decisions." *Personality and Social Psychology Bulletin* 9(4): 551–8.

—— 1986. "Modern Racism, Ambivalence, and the Modern Racism Scale. In *Prejudice, Discrimination, and Racism*, ed. John F. Dovido. San Diego, CA: Academic Press.

McConahay, John B. and Joseph C. Hough. 1976. "Symbolic Racism." *Journal of Social Issues* 32(2): 23–45.

McConahay, John B., Betty B. Hardee, and Valerie Batts. 1981. "Has

Racism Declined in America? It Depends on Who is Asking and What is Asked." *Journal of Conflict Resolution* 25(4): 563–79.

McCoy, Dorian L., Rachelle Winkle-Wagner, and Courtney L. Luedke. 2015. "Colorblind Mentoring? Exploring White Faculty Mentoring of Students of Color." *Journal of Diversity in Higher Education* 8(4): 225–42.

McDermott, Monica. 2015. "Color-Blind and Color-Visible Identity Among American Whites." *American Behavioral Scientist* 59(11): 1452–73.

McNamee, Stephen J. and Robert K. Miller. 2009. *The Meritocracy Myth*. Lanham, PA: Rowman & Littlefield.

Magubane, Zine, 2016. "American Sociology's Racial Ontology: Remembering Slavery, Deconstructing Modernity, and Charting the Future of Global Historical Sociology." *Cultural Sociology* 10(3): 369–84.

Malat, Jennifer, Rose Clark-Hitt, Diana Jill Burgess, Greta Friedemann-Sanchez, and Michelle Van Ryn. 2010. "White Doctors and Nurses On Racial Inequality in Health Care in the USA: Whiteness and Colour-Blind Racial Ideology." *Ethnic and Racial Studies* 33: 1431–50.

Manning, Alex, Douglas Hartmann, and Joseph Gerteis. 2015. "Colorblindness in Black and White: An Analysis of Core Tenets, Configurations, and Complexities." *Sociology of Race and Ethnicity* 1(4): 532–46.

Marker, Emily. 2015. "Obscuring Race: Franco-African Conversations about Colonial Reform and Racism after World War II and the Making of Colorblind France, 1945–1950." *French Politics, Culture and Society* 33(3): 1–23.

Massey, Douglas S. and Denton, Nancy A. 1993. *American Apartheid: Segregation and the Making of the Underclass*. Cambridge, MA: Harvard University Press.

Mayorga-Gallo, Sarah. 2016. "Racism without Racists." *The Wiley Blackwell Encyclopedia of Race, Ethnicity, and Nationalism*, eds. J. Stone, R. Dennis, P. Rizova, A. Smith, and X. Hou.

Mendenhall, Ruby, Nicole M. Brown, and Michael L. Black. 2017. "The Potential of Big Data in Rescuing and Recovering Black Women's Contributions to the Du Bois-Atlanta School and to American Sociology." *Ethnic and Racial Studies* 40(8): 1231–3.

Modica, Marianne. 2015. "Unpacking the 'Colorblind Approach':

Accusations of Racism at a Friendly, Mixed-Race School." *Race Ethnicity and Education* 18(3): 396–418.

Monnat, Shannon M. 2010. "The Color of Welfare Sanctioning: Exploring the Individual and Contextual Roles of Race On TANF Case Closures and Benefit Reductions." *Sociological Quarterly* 51: 678–707.

Moras, Amanda. 2010. "Colour-Blind Discourses in Paid Domestic Work: Foreignness and the Delineation of Alternative Racial Markers." *Ethnic and Racial Studies* 33: 233–52.

Morris, A., 2015. *The Scholar Denied: WEB Du Bois and the Birth of Modern Sociology.* California: University of California Press.

Mueller, Jennifer C. 2017. "Producing Colorblindness: Everyday Mechanisms of White Ignorance." *Social Problems* 64(2): 219–38.

Myers, Kristen A. 2005. *Racetalk: Racism Hiding in Plain Sight.* Lanham, PA: Rowman & Littlefield.

Neville, Helen A., Roderick L. Lilly, Georgia Duran, Richard M. Lee, and LaVonne Browne. 2000. "Construction and Initial Validation of the Color-Blind Racial Attitudes Scale (CoBRAS)." *Journal of Counseling Psychology* 47: 59–70.

Neville, Helen A., M. Nikki Coleman, Jameca Woody Falconer, and Deadre Holmes. 2005. "Color-Blind Racial Ideology and Psychological False Consciousness among African Americans." *Journal of Black Psychology* 31(1): 27–45.

Nopper, Tamara K. 2010. "Colorblind Racism and Institutional Actors' Explanations of Korean Immigrant Entrepreneurship." *Critical Sociology* 36: 65–85.

Norton, Michael I., Samuel R. Sommers, Evan P. Apfelbaum, Natassia Pura, and Dan Ariely. 2006. "Color Blindness and Interracial Interaction: Playing the Political Correctness Game." *Psychological Science* 17: 949–53.

O'Brien, Eileen. 2000. "Are We Supposed to be Colorblind or Not? Competing Frames Used by Whites Against Racism." *Race and Society* 3(1): 41–59.

———— 2008. *The Racial Middle: Latinos and Asian Americans Living beyond the Racial Divide.* New York: New York University Press.

Oliver, Melvin L. and Thomas M. Shapiro. 2006. *Black Wealth, White Wealth: A New Perspective on Racial Inequality.* Burlington, MA: Taylor & Francis, 2006.

Omi, Michael and Howard Winant. 2009. "Thinking through Race and Racism." *Contemporary Sociology* 38(2): 121–5.

———— [1986] 2015. *Racial Formation in the United States: From the 1960s to the1990s.* New York: Routledge.

Oware, Matthew. 2016. "'We Stick Out Like a Sore Thumb...' Underground White Rappers' Hegemonic Masculinity and Racial Evasion." *Sociology of Race and Ethnicity* 2(3): 372–86.

Patton, Tracey Owen. 2004. "In the Guise of Civility: The Complicitous Maintenance of Inferential Forms of Sexism and Racism in Higher Education." *Women's Studies in Communication* 27: 60–87.

Pendakur, Vijay. 2015. "Primed to Be Color-Blind." pp. 185–202 in *Killing the Model Minority Stereotype: Asian American Counterstories and Complicity,* eds. Nicholas D. Hartlep and Bradley J. Portfilio. Charlotte, NC: Information Age Publishing.

Pérez, Raúl. 2013. "Learning to Make Racism Funny in the 'Color-Blind' Era: Stand-Up Comedy Students, Performance Strategies, and the (Re)Production of Racist Jokes in Public." *Discourse and Society* 24: 478–503.

———— 2017. "Racism Without Hatred? The Prevalence of Racist Humor in the 'Colorblind' Era." *Sociological Perspectives* 60(5): 956–974.

Pettigrew, Thomas F. 1979. "Racial Change and Social Policy." *Annals of the American Academy of Political and Social Science* 441(1): 114–31.

Pettigrew, Thomas F. and Roel W. Meertens. 1995. "Subtle and Blatant Prejudice in Western Europe." *European Journal of Social Psychology* 25(1): 57–75.

Pew Research Center. 2016. *News Use Across Social Media Platforms 2016.* Retrieved September 26, 2017 (file:///Users/mburke/Desktop/PJ_2016.05.26_social-media-and-news_FINAL-1.pdf).

Picca, Leslie Houts and Joe R. Feagin. 2007. *Two-Faced Racism: Whites in the Backstage and Frontstage.* New York: Routledge.

Quadagno, Jill. 1994. *The Color of Welfare: How Racism Undermined the War on Poverty.* New York: Oxford University Press.

Ramsaran, Dave. 2009. "Class and the Color-Line in a Changing America." *Race, Gender, and Class* 16: 271–94.

Rhodes, James. 2009. "Revisiting the 2001 Riots: New Labour and the Rise of 'Colour Blind Racism'." *Sociological Research Online* 14: 3.

Rodriquez, Jason. 2006. "Color-Blind Ideology and the Cultural

Appropriation of Hip-Hop." *Journal of Contemporary Ethnography* 35: 645–68.

Roediger, David R. 2008. *How Race Survived US History: From Settlement and Slavery to the Obama Phenomenon.* London: Verso Books.

Schlesinger, Traci. 2011. "The Failure of Race Neutral Policies: How Mandatory Terms and Sentencing Enhancements Contribute to Mass Racialized Incarceration." *Crime and Delinquency* 57: 56–81.

Sears, David O. and Donald R. Kinder. 1971. "Racial Tensions and Voting in Los Angeles," pp. 51–88 in *Los Angeles: Viability and Prospects for Metropolitan Leadership*, ed. Werner Z. Hirsch. New York: Praeger.

Sears, David O. and John B. McConahay. 1973. *The Politics of Violence: The New Urban Blacks and the Watts Riot.* Boston: Houghton-Mifflin.

Selod, Saher. 2015. "Citizenship Denied: The Racialization of Muslim American Men and Women Post-9/11." *Critical Sociology* 41(1): 77–95.

Shelton, Jason E. and M. Nicole Coleman. 2009. "After the Storm: How Race, Class, and Immigration Concerns Influenced Beliefs About the Katrina Evacuees." *Social Science Quarterly* 90: 480–96.

Smith, Candis Watts and Sarah Mayorga-Gallo. 2017. "The New Principle–Policy Gap: How Diversity Ideology Subverts Diversity Initiatives." *Sociological Perspectives* 60(5): 889–911.

Smith, Dorothy E. 1990. *The Conceptual Practices of Power: A Feminist Sociology of Knowledge.* Toronto: University of Toronto Press.

——— 2005. *Institutional Ethnography: A Sociology for People.* Lanham, PA: AltaMira Press.

Smith, Robert Charles. 1995. *Racism in the Post-Civil Rights Era: Now You See It, Now You Don't.* New York: SUNY Press.

Sniderman, Paul M., Thomas Piazza, Philip E. Tetlock, and Ann Kendrick. 1991. "The New Racism." *American Journal of Political Science* 35(2): 423–47.

Southern Poverty Law Center. 2016. *Ten Days After: Harassment and Intimidation in the Aftermath of the Election.* Retrieved June 7, 2017. (https://www.splcenter.org/sites/default/files/com_hate_incidents_report_final.pdf)

——— 2017. Hate Map. Retrieved September 14, 2017. (https://www.splcenter.org/hate-map)

Stoll, Laurie Cooper. 2013. *Race and Gender in the Classroom: Teachers, Privilege, the Conceptual Practices of Power and Enduring Social Inequalities.* Lanham, PA: Lexington Books.

Sweeney, Kathryn A. 2006. "The Blame Game: Racialized Responses to Hurricane Katrina." *Du Bois Review* 3: 161–74.

Tatum, Beverly Daniel. 1997. *Why Are All the Black Kids Sitting Together in the Cafeteria? And Other Conversations About Race.* New York: Basic Books.

Tatum, Katharine and Irene Brown. 2016. "Colour-blind, Colour-visible or Colour-frustrated? Dominican Immigrants in Atlanta Accepting and Rejecting US Racial Ideologies." Presented at the Annual Meeting of the American Sociological Association, Seattle, WA.

Tesler, Michael. 2012. "The Return of Old-Fashioned Racism to White Americans' Partisan Preferences in the Early Obama Era." *Journal of Politics* 75(1): 110–23.

Treitler, Vilna Bashi. 2014. "Introduction: Race Is a Fiction... Coloring Children and Parents Nonetheless," pp. 1–20 in *Race in Transnational and Transracial Adoption,* ed. Vilna Bashi Treitler. New York: Palgrave Macmillan.

Unzueta, Miguel M., Brian S. Lowery, and Eric D. Knowles. 2008 "How Believing in Affirmative Action Quotas Protects White Men's Self-Esteem." *Organizational Behavior and Human Decision Processes* 105(1): 1–13.

Vargas, Nicholas. 2014. "Off White: Colour-blind Ideology at the Margins of Whiteness." *Ethnic and Racial Studies* 37(13): 2281–302.

Vasquez, Jessica M. 2014. "Race Cognizance and Colorblindness: Effects of Latino/Non-Hispanic White Intermarriage." *Du Bois Review: Social Science Research on Race* 11(2): 273–93.

Warikoo, Natasha K. and Janine de Novais. 2014. "Colour-Blindness and Diversity: Race Frames and Their Consequences for White Undergraduates at Elite US Universities." *Ethnic and Racial Studies* 38(6): 860–76.

Washington, Mary Helen. 1988. "Introduction," p. xx in *The Schomburg Library of Nineteenth-Century Black Women Writers,* ed. Mary Helen Washington. New York: Oxford University Press.

Welburn, Jessica S. and Cassi L. Pittman. 2012. "Stop 'Blaming the Man': Perceptions of Inequality and Opportunities for Success in the Obama Era Among Middle-Class African Americans." *Ethnic and Racial Studies* 35: 523–40.

Wellman, David T. 1993. *Portraits of White Racism*, 2nd edn. New York, NY: Cambridge University Press.

West, Cornel. 1995. "Foreword." In *Critical Race Theory: The Key Writings that Formed the Movement*, eds. Kimberlé Crenshaw, Neil Gotanda, Gary Peller, and Kendall Thomas. New York: The New Press.

Wilson, William Julius. 1980. *The Declining Significance of Race: Blacks and Changing American Institutions*. Chicago, IL: University of Chicago Press.

―――― 1987. *The Truly Disadvantaged: The Inner City, the Underclass, and Social Policy*. Chicago: University of Chicago Press.

―――― 1996. *When Work Disappears: The World of the New Urban Poor*. New York: Vintage Books.

―――― 2009. *More than Just Race: Being Black and Poor in the Inner City*. New York: W. W. Norton & Company.

Worthington, Roger L., Rachel L. Navarro, Michael Loewy, and Jeni Hart. 2008. "Color-Blind Racial Attitudes, Social Dominance Orientation, Racial-Ethnic Group Membership and College Students' Perceptions of Campus Climate." *Journal of Diversity in Higher Education* 1(1): 8–19.

Zamudio, Margaret M. and Francisco Rios. 2006. "From Traditional to Liberal Racism: Living Racism in the Rveryday." *Sociological Perspectives* 49: 483–501.

Zeskind, Leonard. 2012. "A Nation Dispossessed: The Tea Party Movement and Race." *Critical Sociology* 38(4): 495–509.

Index